Frontis

This extremely evocative photograph by Fred H. Done was
taken at Whatcroft near Northwich on the Trent and Mersey
Canal, on a winter's afternoon in the late 1930s. The boat,
aptly named *Snowflake*, is most probably from the fleet of
Potter and Son of Runcorn. While there was considerable
activity in the 1930s on the Grand Union Canal to modernise
that waterway, in the Midlands and the north trade on the
canals was gradually declining. This picture has won for its
photographer a number of photographic awards before
World War II.

NARROW BOATS AT WORK

Michael E Ware

MOORLAND PUBLISHING CO

© M. E. Ware 1980

ISBN 0 86190 006 5

Photoset by Advertiser
Printers Ltd, Newton Abbot
and printed in Great Britain by
Redwood Burn Ltd,
Trowbridge & Esher for
Moorland Publishing Co Ltd,
PO Box 2, 9-11 Station Street,
Ashbourne, Derbyshire,
DE6 1DZ.

CONTENTS

ACKNOWLEDGEMENTS

In researching illustrations for a book such as this, one has to undertake a tremendous amount of detective work, a great deal of letter writing and a lot of travelling around the country to locate sources. Many people have helped in the production of this book, either by providing illustrations or by giving me a lead as to where they might be found. For example, I was lucky enough to be told of a set of charming photographs mainly taken on the Trent and Mersey Canal by Fred H. Done of Knutsford. Fred Done, now in his 70s was a keen amateur photographer from an early age. Living as he did then in Northwich he was surrounded by canals and found them 'pictorial with human interest and movement, which changed through the seasons'. He sold a number of his canal pictures to local daily papers, and won any number of photographic competitions with them. His set showing salt loading at Anderton (not all used in this book) won a prize in the *Daily Dispatch*. Some were taken on a Kodak Recomar folding camera, others on a heavy Thornton Pickard Reflex.

Now that the wide ranging archives of photographs at the National Railway Museum at York are being sorted out, some excellent canal pictures are coming to light, and I am most grateful to John Edgington for his co-operation in making copies of these available to me. Philip Weaver of Kenilworth actually worked on pairs of trading boats during the 1950s and carried his camera with him. The content and quality of his pictures is superb. Hugh McKnight, as usual, was extremely helpful, allowing me to take away great handfulls of prints, many of which I was subsequently unable to use. Hugh McKnight's library is most comprehensive. Talking of libraries, researchers for canal material should not forget the commercial picture libraries such as Barnaby's, Popperphotos, Keystone etc. A few pictures from these sources have been used in this book. Tony Condor of the Waterways Museum, Stoke Bruerne, follows in the footsteps of Richard Hutchings and is just as long-suffering when dealing with eccentric picture researchers. Sonia Rolt kindly let me look through her late husband's canal photographs, as did the widow of the late E. Temple-Thurston of *Flower of Gloster* fame. I would also like to thank Keith Whetstone of the *Coventry Evening Telegraph* for being so helpful. Dr J. R. Hollick, Ian Wright, Peter Lead, Denys Hutchings and Hugh Potter (of *Waterways World*) all went out of their way to be helpful.

Stan Miles of British Waterways, Devizes, along with some of his Section colleagues took the trouble to visit the author to help identify some of the World War I pictures taken of the Kennet and Avon which had come from the archives of the Imperial War Museum. Kitty Gayford, Margaret Ridout and Mrs Helen Skyrme helped with pictures and identification of some of the World War II photographs. D. R. Hills, Technical Sales Manager of Wolvercote Paper Mills gave up a lot of time to try and trace an elusive picture of narrowboats at that mill, and let me have copies of the wharf clerk's notebooks, detailing costs relating to the haulage of coal by rail and canal to the mill.

Picture postcards are a great source of illustration for a book such as this, many of which come from my own collection, but I have been greatly helped by Alan Robinson founder of the flourishing Canal Card Collectors' Circle.

Three people stand out above the others for the time they have spent with me over this book. I have visited them all, and borrowed lots of pictures, many of which have been used in the book — though often credited to the original source and not to their collections. They have all read the manuscript and offered many helpful pieces of advice and additions. Thank you: Edward Paget-Tomlinson; Alan Faulkner; and David McDougall.

Many of the letters that had to be written during the research period of the book were undertaken by my wife, helped in their spare time by Mrs Doris Draysey and Christine Hodgson. My wife, Janet, gave me great moral support as well as typing the manuscript, at least twice. To the recipients of my many letters, who helped in so many ways and who have not been personally acknowledged, thank you very much. Though I have been helped by many people with this book, I must take the blame if mistakes are found.

The author and publishers are grateful to the following for the use of illustrations: I. Argent, 112; E. Appleton, 165; Black Country Museum, 136, 162; *Birmingham Evening Mail*, 186; Barnaby's Picture Library, 81, 188, 212; Cadbury Brothers Ltd, 36; Canal Cruising Co Ltd, 201-2; *Coventry Evening Telegraph*, 147, 199, 203; F.H. Done, *Frontis*, 20-2, 32, 40, 57, 59, 77, 154; Dudley Canal Trust, 16, 138; Dudley Public Library (Will King Collection), 135; A. Faulkner, 55, 190; G.E.A. Fiddes, 98-9; Fox Photos, 92; Gloucester Libraries, 2; G. Guest, 130; Kitty Gayford, 178-9; D. Gittings, 144; Rose Gill, 14; H. Hanson, 116; Commander H.O. Hill, 78; J. Hollingshead, 155; Hertfordshire County Records Office, 61, 71; S. Hobley, 15; J.R. Hollick, 11, 17-18; Imperial War Museum, 101-3, 105, 117, 146, 172-4, 177, 181-2, 184-5; Kennet & Avon Canal Trust, 176; Keystone Press, 180, 183; Kodak Museum, 69; P. Lead, 145; Leicester Museum, 8; Museum of English Rural Life, 109; D. McDougall, 10, 125; H. McKnight, 26, 47-8, 51, 54, 82, 86, 97, 104, 106, 110-11, 120, 122, 126, 128, 133, 137, 143, 159, 194-8, 200; National Monuments Record, 166-7; Northampton Library, 150-1, 115; National Coal Board, 1; National Railway Museum, 3-4, 118, 142, 157, 161, 170; M. Palmer, 44, 152; L. Porter, 43, 123, 129; Popperfotos, 33; J.G. Parkinson, 13, 121, 139, 168; A. Robinson, 9; L.T.C. Rolt Archive, 30, 58, 107; Rochdale Metropolitan Library, 67; F. Rodgers, 83, 108, 164; W. Russon, 113-14; Mrs Smallwood, 141; E.A. Shearing, 34-5, 76; E. Paget-Tomlinson, 23, 25, 31, 63-4, 87, 148, 193; *Wiltshire Times*, 42; Mrs Temple Thurston, 74, 96, 149; I.L. Wright, 37, 45, 79, 124, 169; C.P. Weaver, 12, 60, 80, 127, 191-2; Waterways Museum, 5-7, 19, 24, 38-9, 46, 49, 50, 53, 62, 73, 84, 88-91, 93, 100, 119, 132, 134, 153, 158, 160, 171, 187. Illustrations not otherwise acknowledged are from the author's collection.

PREFACE

This book is unashamedly about *narrowboats* on the canals of England. The author fully realises that there were many other types of craft trading on the inland waterways of Britain, but he has chosen only to illustrate the narrow-beamed craft, which are now collectively known as long-boats or more commonly narrowboats. Practically all types of inland waterway craft have been illustrated and described in Edward Paget-Tomlinson's recent book *Britain's Canal and River Craft,* also published by Moorland.

The problem with a book such as this which is written around historic photographs is that it is not always possible to illustrate every point the author would like to make; very often suitable illustrations cannot be found. He is, therefore, left to compromise; which means in this case that some of the less common varieties of narrowboats may not be included and possibly some boating techniques have been left out, as have many examples of the different types of cargo carried. Where possible, the illustrations (except in the last chapter) have been chosen from pre-1950 photographs, but with the greater interest in canals since World War II, it was

impossible to ignore some very good post-1950 pictures. Most of these, however, represent the narrowboat at work much as it had been for the last hundred or so years.

The author has found it very hard to find illustrations from a number of northern canals, such as the Rochdale or Huddersfield Narrow. Perhaps pictures do not exist; or it may be that research for them has not been deep enough. Again, the pictures used in the book show boats and techniques which could have been commonly used on these northern waterways.

While there are still pockets of trade by 'Number One's' on the canals, this book is about the days when such trade was commonplace, and people did not stop and stare as 'the boats went by'. Here then for the first time is a full-length picture book devoted entirely to the narrowboat at work.

Note: From 1st January 1929 a group of canals formerly known as The Grand Junction Canal became The Grand Union Canal. Throughout this book the name Grand Union Canal has been used to cover all these waterways, even if the photograph depicted scenes prior to 1929.

INTRODUCTION

The Duke of Bridgewater's Canal from Worsley to Manchester was one of the pioneer canals to be built in Britain. Completed to Stretford in 1761 and to Manchester two years later, it was the brainchild of the duke's agent, John Gilbert, aided and abetted by James Brindley, a skilled millwright. The canal was originally some seven miles long, and allowed coal from the duke's mines to be brought into Manchester much cheaper than if it had been taken over the poor roads of that time by horse and cart, or packhorse. Though this waterway is nowadays termed a wide canal, it is from this first canal that we must try and find the origin of the narrowboat.

The most unusual aspect of the Duke's mines at Worsley was the fact that he used some forty-six miles of underground canals, on three levels, to move the coal from the coalface to the surface. Special boats were developed for use on these underground canals, generally called mine boats or 'Starvationers' because of their exposed knees (ribs). These boats were all 50ft long, but came in three different widths, 4ft 8in, 6ft 4in and 7ft 0in, depending on which part of the mine they were to be used in. All these craft would nowadays be termed narrowboats. In passing, it is also interesting to note that at this early stage, coal was not just dumped into the hold of these boats; it was collected into containers of 5-8cwt each and handled in that way. We sometimes look upon container traffic as being something new. Once the mineboats had come out of the narrow confines of the tunnels, the cargoes were transferred to the larger sized boats which were then lashed end-to-end and towed by horse, in short trains of about six each, to Manchester, where they again entered a tunnel under the city at Deansgate. The containers were then lifted from the boats to the surface, up a deep shaft, by a water-powered crane.

While other traders may have wished to put boats onto the Duke of Bridgewater's canal, he kept all the traffic to himself. He owned a large fleet of boats which, in the main, were of a similar type to those to be found on local rivers. In this case the Mersey flat was the most popular boat which could be sailed on the River Mersey but would have been towed by horse on the inland waterway. Before leaving the mine boats of the Duke of Bridgewater, it is worth mentioning that some thirty or so years later, when the canals of South Wales were being built, craft that were very similar in design to the original mine boats were used. In this case they were all 60ft long, but varied in width from 8ft 6in to 9ft 0in. As the canals of Wales were never connected to the main waterway system, these boats changed very little over the next one hundred and forty years.

While still building the Bridgewater Canal, Brindley was approached by Josiah Wedgewood to build a canal which would connect the River Trent and the River Mersey, and which would pass through Burslem, where he had just built his first pottery. Later this plan

1 Special boats were developed for use on the underground canals at the Worsley collieries. These were generally called 'mine boats' or 'starvationers', and the exposed knees or ribs clearly shown in this picture gave them this name. The picture shows one of the boats being used for maintenance purposes, some forty years after the mines closed in 1887. As can be seen, these original narrowboats were of very simple construction. One means of moving the trains of boats out of the underground tunnels was to create a current so that they flowed out without a great deal of manpower. The structure in this photograph is the sluice gate at the entrance to the mine, which was used to build up a head of water, which when released would cause a current within the mines.

developed into one to link the rivers Thames and Severn also, and join all the canals up in the middle of the country. Having decided on the proposed route of the Trent and Mersey Canal, decisions had to be taken early on as to what dimensions it should be built to. The Bridgewater Canal had been built over relatively flat ground, and so required no locks; the only major engineering feat was Britain's first canal aqueduct at Barton, which carried the waterway over the River Irwell at a height of 38ft above the river. In its day the aqueduct was said to be one of the wonders of Great Britain. The Trent and Mersey Canal, on the other hand, was going to be quite a different propostion. It had to climb up to Kidsgrove and then drop down through Stoke-on-Trent to the valley of the River Trent, and to be completely practical Harecastle Hill, at the summit, would have to be tunnelled through, as it was just not possible to go round or over it. Harecastle Tunnel, 2,880yd long, was Britain's greatest engineering feat at that time, and took seven years to complete.

Brindley must have soon realised that, at that time, it was financially impractical to make this a wide canal, but how narrow should it be? The duke's canal had been built wide enough to take the local Mersey flats, as well as the mine boats. Possibly the bore of Harecastle Tunnel holds a clue. The building of the tunnel had to start at the same time as the rest of the canal building commenced (even so the tunnel was the last part of the canal to be completed). From this it can be seen that the bore of the tunnel had to be decided at the commencement of the design of the waterway. In order to keep the costs down, it was decided that it would be 9ft wide at water level. This means that boats approximately 7ft wide could navigate in this width if they were going very slowly, and as there was to be no towpath in the tunnel, the boats would be legged (walked) through by the crew. This tunnel dimension then fixed the width of the boat and by other calculations, Brindley must have thought 25 tons of cargo in one boat to be a reasonable amount. The depth of the waterway controlled the draught of the boat and through this the total payload. He may well have thought that the larger the Duke of Bridgewater's mine boats was nearing the size of craft that he felt adequate for the canals, but in order to increase its carrying capacity, the length would have to be increased also. To use a generalisation, Brindley built his locks to the size 72ft by 7ft which meant that they could take narrowboats up to 70ft long by 6ft 10in wide.

Who, then, built the first boats? There were obviously no boatyards at inland places such as Middlewich, Stoke-on-Trent or Rugeley at that time. We can only assume, therefore, that boats were built by local craftsmen, such as blacksmiths, wheelwrights, carpenters and similar versatile people, and it is not unreasonable to assume that some of the first canal craft were built on the bank of the waterway by people such as these. As to design, they had the mine boats as a guide (if they needed one), and as they had a restriction in length, it was obvious that the fine bow and stern lines of the mine boats could not be repeated if maximum cargo-carrying capacity was required. From this we can easily deduce that right from the start the boats on the narrow canals had the narrow gutted bow and stern which have been seen on the narrowboat for the last 200 years. Gradually, over the years, some of the major differences from these individual boat building places have been eliminated; hence, to the non-enthusiast at any rate, most narrowboats have looked roughly alike over the last hundred years, or so. It is very difficult to take seriously some of the really early illustrations which exist of waterway craft, as they are clearly very inaccurate, and in many cases could not have floated at all! Some of the earliest narrowboat pictures which are thought to have been accurately portrayed were by Shepherd in 1828, and these have been reproduced many times. Although these were engraved 62 years after the starting of the Trent and Mersey Canal they do show narrowboats very much as we have come to know them today.

In general terms, Brindley's original dimensions for a lock and a tunnel (the features which govern everything to do with width or length on a waterway) have influenced canal building in the Midlands and in areas where waterways did not have direct access to seagoing craft. Some canals were, however, built to a wider dimension, and were known as barge canals, because it was hoped that they would attract trade from river craft, ie keels and flats. Many of these types of boats were around 70ft long anyway, which meant that the narrowboat could also trade over the barge canals. The majority of the barge canals were wide enough to allow two narrowboats into a lock side by side, which was a very useful feature, particularly as on wide waterways a horse could often tow two boats. This was also useful with the coming of the motorboat, which nearly always towed an unpowered craft (butty). An exception was the Leeds and Liverpool Canal, which was built to cater for the Yorkshire keel, and while the locks on this canal were wide, they were only 62ft long, which precluded full length narrowboats right from the start, hence they developed their own style of short boat.

Originally, narrowboats were constructed completely in wood, as this was the natural material of ship-building and was readily available; and it was the natural material of the people from the land who were building them. Though metal boats were experimented with, they did not become popular until this century. There was a halfway stage when composite boats were made with metal sides and wooden bottoms. The coming of powered craft tended to speed up the change to all-metal construction, but many wooden horse-drawn boats were very successfully converted to power without too many problems.

There are no firm facts to give us the origins of the narrowboat, neither is there any easy way to find out who were the first boatmen. As with the travellers on the fairground, the boatmen did not like the term 'gypsy'; while many people may think that the boatmen originated from this source, reasearch has shown that only a very small percentage are likely to have forsaken the nomadic life of the land for one on water. Some people, looking into the back of the cabin of a narrowboat, have remarked on the similarity in layout to that of a gypsy caravan, so continuing the myth of the gypsy origin. Because of the state of roads in this country, gypsies did not, however, have caravans until well into the 1800s; they lived under canvas instead. It is very likely that boatmen were forced, for various reasons, to make their craft family boats long before the advent of the gypsy caravan. If anyone copied anyone, it was the gypsies who copied the boatmen.

Perhaps we can gain some idea of who might have been the first boatmen if we look at those people who would have been around the newly dug canals, and, in particular, those who might have lost their jobs because of them. While overland trade and transport was not good until the coming of the canals, there were carriers or carters who specialised in the carriage of goods. They carried goods either by wagon or by packhorse. It would seem fairly clear that those people would have seen the canals as a definite threat to their livelihood and could well have become boatmen in the first instance. Many carters and waggoners may well have been involved with working for the canal contractors when the canals were being built; as a result of this, they may have lost some of their previous contracts. Small tenant farmers who were just scratching a living may well have joined the ranks of boatmen as well. They would have all been used to hard work in the open air and would have worked with horses and been involved with haulage, all part of the boatman's life. If we add into the cross-section of the eighteenth-century population, some ex-canal navvies (very few of them Irish) who had no wish to move on to the next job, or who had settled locally, plus some river boatmen where the canals were close to this type of waterway, you will get some idea of the many types of people who could have made up the first narrow-boating communities. In the first instance, most of the crews were male, usually one man and a boy. Because there were not that many canals, and inland trade was still developing, many of the journeys were relatively short, so that the boatman usually lived in a house, returning home fairly frequently, as he was never very far from his home. As the canals developed, and as trade spread all over the country, so the journeys made by the boatman were longer, and for this reason, he had to spend more time away from home. It therefore seems quite logical that the boatman would have wanted to take his wife with him on his boat, and, particularly after the depression of 1815, it was more sensible to do away with the boy and use the wife instead, as unpaid help. Here then we see the start of family boating and the requirement of the narrowboat to be fitted with a cabin. Where possible, the boatman also used his children, often using one of them to walk with the horse. Later, with the coming of the railways and the competition produced by them, it was almost essential that the narrowboat became a family boat, and the luxury of paid hands became very rare. The hours worked by the boatman were extremely long, and his only contact with the rest of civilisation came when he was at a wharf loading or unloading, and when he had to go shopping.

It was this isolation on the boats which kept the boatmen away from community life and tended to give them the description 'a race apart'. Gradually they interbred; this was quite natural, as they were, in the main, only mixing with their own kind. Continually standing in close proximity to the smoke from the cabin's stove, must have increased the swarthy look which they obtained through living and working in the open air. Another reason for the myth that the boatmen stemmed from gypsy stock.

The author has dwelt for some length on how the canal system came into being, and how he feels the narrowboat evolved, and has given some indication of the type of people who may have made the first boatmen. Many books have been written outlining the complicated history of the British canal system, but for the reader to fully understand why there are virtually no traditional narrowboats trading on the canals today, a brief look at some of the more important milestones is required. Even while Brindley was helping to build the Bridgewater Canal, and planning the Trent and Mersey many other canal proposals were put forward and the years between the 1770s and 1800 were the times of real 'canal mania' and canal building in Britain. It seemed that every town or village which had any form of industry wanted a canal. The latter part of the eighteenth century and the early decades of the nineteenth century were the real heydays of the canal. While road transport improved through the 1800s with the setting up of turnpike trusts, long haul overland transport by road was often still difficult, as many parishes did not keep up their roads. The canals had the carriage of goods all their own way until the railways started to spread across the country from the 1840s onwards. Like the canals, the railways were only of maximum use to industry if there was a railway line from the supplier's premises to the user's premises. Any transhipment of the goods was an added expense. The railways were supreme at carrying passengers, though it must not be forgotten that for many years the canal companies also carried people, as well as goods. The railways were also very good at delivering relatively small loads of goods to rural communities, via the pick-up goods train. There were many instances where goods were carried by water from factory to railway siding for onward transmission by rail, because the final destination was rail connected but not water connected. Similarly, the railways brought in goods to canals for places that had water facilities but no railway lines. Where speed was essential, then the railway usually scored, but where industry required a regular supply of raw materials the canals were able to under-cut the railways for many years. Gradually, during the latter part of the nineteenth century, the railway competition caused the canal companies' trade to decrease. Originally each canal was privately owned; gradually some of these came together into larger groups, or were even taken over by the railways. Surprisingly, the railways kept many of them open, but usually let them decline, and, in many cases, they operated at a loss. For a better idea of the reasons for the closure of many of the canals, the author's previous two-volumed work *Britain's Lost Waterways* gives detailed explanations.

While the canal system gradually contracted, carrying by narrowboat was still taking place in great quantities to and from, and in and around, industrial areas. During World War I many boatmen left the canals, not to return. During the 1920s and '30s road transport really came into its own, and the roads took trade both from the railways and the canals. During the latter part of this period, one combine, The Grand Union Canal Company had a final fling, spending over a million pounds improving the canal between London and Birmingham, and building up a very large fleet of new boats for carrying cargo. Surprisingly, this was done without a great injection of Government money. The company borrowed the money, but the Government did help with a grant towards the interest of the funds to modernise the canal, but the company received no Government help for the purchase of boats. While the carrying company never made any real profit, its losses were small in the context of the Grand Union Canal Company's overall operations. In 1948 most of the canals and some of the fleets of boats were nationalised and it is often erroneously thought that this was the end of carrying in quantity. It was not. The 1950s saw a great deal of cargo being carried, both by British Waterways, fleet carriers, and the independent 'number ones' as the owner-boatmen were called. The real death knell came in the early 1960s with the wholesale slaughter of fleets of narrowboats by the scrapman, or by scuttling.

The Inland Waterways Association was formed in 1946 and, gradually, through their endeavour, the plight of the canal has been brought to a wider audience. The result is that more and more people are turning to the canals for leisure purposes, though the Association has always tried to foster the use of canals for commercial carrying as well. In the early days of pleasure cruising many of the boats were converted working narrowboats, and this is touched on in the last chapter of this book. Briefly, and in very general terms, this was the background to the canal system on which the narrowboat traded. It is hoped that this book will give the reader some insight into the workings of these boats, the cargoes they carried, and the people who lived aboard.

1 DOCKS AND WHARVES

2   Docks or inland ports were usually built where a canal
ran to a major river or to the sea. Here cargoes could be
transhipped or stored. Those canals which ran into the River
Severn had the disadvantage that parts of that river,
particularly the stretch between Gloucester and Berkeley Pill
(near Sharpness) were very treacherous pieces of water and
could only be navigated by large craft on very high tides.
This meant that it was very difficult for cargoes originating
in Birmingham or the Black Country, for example, to reach
ocean going vessels. On 26 April 1827 the Gloucester and
Berkeley Ship Canal was opened to avoid this bad stretch of
the river and cargoes could now be transhipped in
Gloucester Docks. Here, in the days of sail, not a steamer is
in sight, and narrowboats from the fleet of the Severn and
Canal Carrying Co Ltd are loading and unloading. In the
foreground is a square sterned Severn Trow, one of the
smaller trading vessels which operated on the River Severn
and linking waterways.

3 The small hamlet of Netherpool on the Wirral Penninsular gradually developed into one of the principal canal ports of Great Britain. From 1797 onwards it was known as Ellesmere Port. It was Thomas Telford who was first responsible for seeing the opportunities here, as the River Mersey was much easier to navigate than the nearby River Dee, which was rapidly silting up; with the opening of the Birmingham and Liverpool Junction Canal in 1835, Ellesmere Port became even more important, and was further helped by the Manchester Ship Canal which opened officially on 21 May 1894. Various specialised wharves existed within the port complex. A plan of 1910 lists, for example, timber wharf, flint wharf (and another flint and clay wharf), grain warehouses, china clay warehouses, iron shed and an iron ore wharf. By the 1880s one of the major trades was in pig iron; this came in aboard coasters and was transhipped into narrowboats for onward transmission to Staffordshire and the Black Country. This picture, about 1900, shows the iron ore wharf with narrowboats loading, the nearest one being from the fleet of W. Foster of Tipton. The steam vessel on the outside of the two on the left is the tug *Arrow* which was used for towing flats and barges on the River. *Arrow* was built in 1889 at Dundee for the Shropshire Union and registered at Chester. The other vessel is a paddle driven tug, probably the *Lord Clive* built in 1875 and acquired by the Shropshire Union in 1904. Her hull was still in existence, in use as a dumb barge, at Liverpool in the 1960s. The coal drop behind the two steamers had been removed by 1924.

4 While the original docks at Ellesmere Port were at the same level as the canal to Chester, the rest of the complex were later built two locks lower, with a third lock leading into the River Mersey. This view of about 1900, was taken below the first lock down from the Shropshire Union Canal, and shows one of that canal company's flats unloading pipes while actually moored in the lock; surely a most unusual practice on a busy waterway? On the right the crew of a Shropshire Union Railway and Canal Company narrowboat have not stopped to pose for the photographer, but have continued working the lock. Behind can be seen the very decorative lighthouse marking the entrance to the port from the River Mersey, but latterly from the Ship Canal. It is now a listed building. On the left is the main warehouse of the port with the sea-going ships on the far side of it. One of the famous hydraulic powered cranes can be seen affixed to the side of the warehouse. The gas lamps on the wharfside were supplied with gas by the Shropshire Union Company's own gasworks.

4

6   One of the advantages of docks such as the Regent's Canal Dock was that cargo could be loaded overside and directly into the holds of waiting narrow boats. Unloading of exports could be carried out the same way. This cuts out time-wasting and the expense of unloading onto the dockside and subsequently re-loading into boats. Here in the late 1930s a pair of boats from the Grand Union Canal Carrying Co are seen loading drums of paint or creosote overside. It would appear that the water is low in the dock, no doubt due to maintenance work being carried out below normal water level. The River Thames outside the entrance locks to these docks was, of course, tidal.

5   London's largest dock directly connected to the canal system was Regent's Canal Dock; this in turn lead into the Regent's Canal and the Paddington arm, both sections of the Grand Union Canal, and thence to the Midlands. All types of cargo came into this dock, but in latter years the principle ones were coal, metals and timber. These wide Thames lighters worked through the large sized locks on the Regent's Canal and also out on to the lower reaches of the Grand Union Canal itself. The coal and timber was local traffic for installations within a few miles' radius of the canal. Much coal was used by canalside power stations such as Marylebone, but this traffic declined when electricity generating became more centralised at stations such as Battersea and later Bankside. Thames lighters, of course, took large quantities of cargo up the Thames to the many riverside wharves which existed at this time. Long haul traffic would have been taken by narrow boat such as the ones seen loaded and sheeted up in the background. The steamer belonged to the General Steam Navigation Company, and is *Petrel* (built in 1920); she was sunk by a 'U' boat in September 1941.

CHEDDLETON, NR. LEEK

7 In 1929 the Grand Union Canal Co Ltd came into being as an amalgamation of five other companies. This new company realised that trade would have to be tempted back onto the canals, and they set about building a very large fleet of narrowboats for their expected traffic. Many new cargoes were found, and just before the last war their carrying subsidiary, the Grand Union Canal Carrying Co had a fleet of just over 370 boats. The company only made a profit on its carrying fleet during World War II; at other times it lost money. Here a group of loaded boats wait for customs clearance before leaving Regent's Canal Dock for the Midlands, with a cargo of steel.

8 The famous carrying company of Fellows Morton & Clayton had a depot in Leicester, seen here around the turn of this century. It looks as if the steam powered narrowboat *Earl* has just arrived, possibly after running almost non-stop from London. The boat is being unloaded onto the horse and cart alongside, either for direct delivery to a local firm, or for storage in the Fellows Morton & Clayton warehouse. Barrels from the American Glucose Co litter the wharf. This is a charming period photograph showing how the area would have been lit by gas. The different styles of wharf cranes are also absolutely typical. This, then, was a typical well-organised inland wharf. *Earl* was the last steam narrowboat to trade (see later chapter for details of the steamers) only going out of commission in 1931. She was the last wooden steamer to be built at Saltley Dock in June 1895, and she was sold to another carrier in 1925. The masthead style of lamp at the bow would have been lit for use in tunnels and also for night runs.

9 On the other hand, country wharves would be different. A busy scene at the village wharf at Cheddleton, near Leek, on the Caldon Branch of the Trent and Mersey Canal, about 1905. Just leaving the lock is a boat loaded with limestone which had come from the big Cauldon Low quarries above Froghall. Approaching the lock is the narrowboat *Perseverance* owned by a trader from Middlewich. This boat is empty and is most probably making for Froghall to load lime or limestone. Much of the limestone from Froghall went to the blast furnaces in the Black Country, particularly Hickman's at Bilston. The boat *Success* alongside the wharf may be waiting to load bricks from the pile on the wharf, or has just brought them. The boat in the immediate foreground is an old wooden ice breaker which was based at Cheddleton at this time.

10 This scene at a country wharf at Aynho on the Southern Oxford Canal would have been typical of the heyday of canals, even though this picture was taken in 1905. One boat at the wharfside is unloading coal, which is being taken by wheelbarrow to the coal pile on the right of the photograph. The other boat is unloading road stone, which is being taken away by horse and cart to other dumps or for use on a local road. Passing the wharf is an empty horse-drawn boat proceeding northwards. Where boats to be unloaded were carrying perishable cargoes, such as wheat or corn, they would use the under cover loading facilities provided by the warehouse on the left of the wharf. It is noticeable also that the towpath is in extremely good condition. This wharf is now the base for a fleet of hire cruisers.

11 Froghall Wharf, the terminus of the Caldon Canal, was a busy place, with both limestone and burnt lime being the main cargoes. The limestone came from the quarries down a 3½ mile tramway, which, as can be seen, terminated on the wharfside. The stone was loaded into the boats by hand from the trucks. To the right was a shed containing lime; this was taken along the raised tramway in the background where it could be loaded direct into boats waiting under the tracks. The huge limekilns are away to the right of the picture. This whole area has now been landscaped to form a picnic site, and it is virtually impossible to imagine it in its working hey-day.

12 Some wharves were hardly wharves at all. Boats were expected to tie up against the bank and unload. In many cases it was difficult to tie alongside, as the water was not deep enough. No wonder canals lost their traffic in competition with other forms of transport. This is the Co-op Wharf at Banbury, and *Python* and *Fazeley* are unloading timber they have brought from Brentford. They have brought their cargo up the Grand Union Canal to Braunston, and then down the Southern Oxford Canal, rather than take it up the Thames to Oxford and then up the lower part of the Southern Oxford Canal which by that time (July 1958) was not used a great deal by trading boats. The narrowboat moored below the timber wharf is *Admiral* of the Samuel Barlow Coal Co Ltd, which, with its butty *Mosquito*, had just delivered to the Co-op forty-four tons of coal from Griff Colliery, Bedworth.

10

12

13

14

13 Right up until the end of commercial carrying the unloading facilities at certain wharves remained primitive in the extreme. Here on the Caldon Canal in the Potteries on a July day in 1958, Roland Barrett and Bill Brooks are seen unloading pottery materials by hand. This is the ex-Anderton Company narrowboat *Nora,* relegated at this time to acting as a day boat by taking materials from Cockshute siding in Stoke, to Harrisons Pottery in Hanley. 1958 was the year when both the Anderton and Mersey Weaver Fleets were sold to British Waterways.

14 The shovel and wheelbarrow were the only standard unloading tools at many wharves. This photograph was taken in the early 1960s at Bullers Wharf in the Potteries, and shows Jack Tolley, Joe Hollingshead and Rose Tolley all helping to unload the motorboat *Anson* and butty *Keppel.* On some boats a wheelbarrow was carried as standard equipment. This pair would have loaded feldspar at Weston Point Docks, travelled up the River Weaver, up the Anderton Lift, and then on up the Trent and Mersey Canal, through Harecastle Tunnel to Stoke-on-Trent. The nearer boat is the *Keppel* one of the Admiral class built for the Docks and Inland Waterway Executive in 1960. On these boats the cloths which covered the cargo if it was perishable were spread over hoops across the hold, and held in place by wedges, which can be seen clearly in this picture.

15 When mechanisation came, it was often crude. Here, in the 1950s, feldspar is being loaded into an Anderton Co motorboat at Weston Point Docks. The feldspar has come from a sea-going ship which has unloaded onto the dockside. Now this large bucket is loaded by hand on the dockside, and swung into the hold of the narrowboat by crane, where it will be manhandled and tipped, since it pivoted about its handle. Cargoes such as these were loaded into two or three distinct piles in the hold, in order to spread the load evenly. Heavy cargoes which would not fill the entire hold would be loaded in 'rucks' leaving spaces between, making it easier to unload. The more 'rucks' the greater the number of shovellers who could unload the boat at the same time. The last regular traffic by canal from Weston Point Docks to the Potteries ended in 1969, when the pottery firm of Dolbeys went into liquidation.

15

16 Gravity was often employed for loading cargoes into boats, but often they had to be unloaded by hand at the other end. Occasionally with cargoes such as grain a form of suction unloading was developed. Here, at Ashwood Basin on the Staffordshire and Worcestershire Canal, boats are being loaded with coal down a shute direct from the railway wagons above. It was also possible to load by taking the boat under the covered section at the end of the arm. This coal came from the Earl of Dudley's own mines, in his own trucks, hence the 'E D' on the wagons. The railway was the Kingswinford Railway financed by Lord Dudley and John Foster, an ironmaster of Stourbridge. The picture is thought to have been taken in 1927. This branch is now a marina. The stone blocks which made up part of the wall on the left are stone sleepers made redundant when the original fish-bellied rails of the standard gauge railway were replaced by bull-head rails about 1860.

16

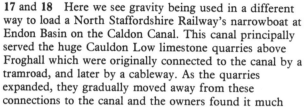

17 and **18**   Here we see gravity being used in a different way to load a North Staffordshire Railway's narrowboat at Endon Basin on the Caldon Canal. This canal principally served the huge Cauldon Low limestone quarries above Froghall which were originally connected to the canal by a tramroad, and later by a cableway. As the quarries expanded, they gradually moved away from these connections to the canal and the owners found it much easier to take the limestone by rail for transhipment at Endon. The railway trucks are side loaders; they are gripped by this special tipping machine, tilted, and the limestone falls into the hoppers, from whence it can be dropped in a more controlled way into the waiting boats. When loading cargoes of this sort, great care had to be taken not to damage the boat.

19, 20, 21, 22 and **23** At Anderton in Cheshire, the Trent and Mersey Canal follows a line 50ft above the River Weaver. The Weaver connects with major docks for sea-going craft such as Weston Point, and it also connects with the open sea. From relatively early times in the history of the Trent and Mersey Canal, attempts were made at transhipment at Anderton to the river below. The easiest product to move in this way was salt, which came loose from the salt works around Middlewich to Anderton, where it was laboriously unloaded into carts, moved over to a series of chutes which connected with the river-going craft below. Completed in 1875, the great Anderton Lift provided a physical connection between the two waterways. Suspended within the lift were two caissons each capable of taking a pair of narrowboats, and they were lowered or raised as required by hydraulic power. By the turn of this century salt and chemicals in the water of the River Weaver had taken their toll of the hydraulic cylinders. Between 1906 and 1908 the lift was converted to electric power. Figure 19 shows the lift prior to its conversion to electricity. The position of the salt chutes alongside are clearly shown. Figures 20-22 show the transfer of salt in the 1930s, from a Henry Seddon of Middlewich narrowboat to a Henry Seddon steam packet below. What hot and thirsty work this must have been! Amazingly the salt chutes continued in use until 1940. After that date refined salt was bagged by the salt companies at the works and it was therefore much more sensible for the cargo to be transhipped overside on the River Weaver, the narroboats having descended using the lift. Such a scene is shown in 1956 (Fig 23) with the dumb barge *Gowanburn* of the Seddon fleet being loaded from a pair of Seddon narrowboats just below the lift. As well as chutes for salt there were also hoists for crated pottery, some of which were steam powered. The reason for the continued used of these chutes must have been to avoid paying a fee for the use of the lift, both down and up again, and possibly a toll on the river itself. The steam flat on the left is the *Weaver Belle*.

20

21

22

23

24 As the Grand Union Canal Carrying Co expanded its carrying potential, the parent company had to expand its wharfside facilities. Sampson Road Wharf, or Birmingham Quay as it was often called, was typical. In 1938 a brand new warehouse was built where boats with perishable cargoes could unload under cover. The wharf around was modernised, new cranes purchased, and this bustling scene would have been typical. Rolls of corrugated cardboard are being unloaded from the butty *Kew* on the left. The rest of her cargo consists of cardboard boxes packed flat. In the foreground are the motorboat *Baldock* and the butty *Banbury*. Motorboat *Stanton* has been partly unloaded. The two life buoys were a requirement if the boats were to trade out onto the tidal River Thames at Brentford. Behind are the butty *Ra* and the motorboat *Fornax*.

25

25 The firm of A. Wander & Co, better known for their product Ovaltine, used to obtain all the coal for the boilers of their factory at Kings Langley by water. Here the butty *Enid* and motorboat *William* are seen being unloaded by an elaborate overhead gantry crane. This factory opened in 1926 and was described as Wander's 'new model factory' — hence the efficient unloading equipment. Unloading by this type of crane was obviously much quicker than by hand, but it required a careful crane driver, so that the grab did not damage the side of the boat or the knees, as it dropped into the hold. *Enid* has been fitted with slack boards in front of the cabin to enable the coal to be piled higher at the stern to take advantage of the extra free board gained by the cabin space. The photograph was taken on 9 April 1956.

26 Warehousing was also an important part of a canal company's function. It was not always possible to unload a boat directly into a factory. The company had to have its own wharves at which goods could be stored until the customer could collect, or the canal carrying company could deliver. In the case of the transhipment dock at the Fellows Morton & Clayton depot at Braunston, this was a stopping point for the fast steam narrowboat service from London. Because the locks from here on to Birmingham were narrow (up until 1934 that is), the steamers dropped their towed butties here, and either continued on solo or they unloaded into the warehouse. This photograph, thought to have been taken in 1910, shows a laden butty lying alongside the wharf under a typical hand operated crane. Beside the butty a steamer can just be seen. Fellows Morton & Clayton specialised in the carrying of pricey cargoes, and good quality foodstuffs was one of these.

27 This publicity picture for Bedford Motors was taken in early 1939. In order to compete with other forms of transport it was necessary for canal companies to be able to collect goods from factories and to deliver them to the client at the end of the trip; in other words, they had to give a 'door-to-door' service. Hence the Grand Union Canal Co owned a fleet of lorries. They were not alone in this; for many years land carriers had horses and carts before the lorry, and photographs exist of lorries in the colours of the Severn and Canal Carrying Co, the Rochdale Canal Co and Fellows Morton & Clayton. Here, narrowboat *Thaxted* (built in 1937) is seen waiting a cargo at Birmingham's Sampson Road Wharf. The unusual liner-type funnel was a feature of some Grand Union Canal Carrying Co boats of the 1930s built by Yarwood. It is likely that the butty alongside is *Taunton*. Behind are *Hadley* and *Hagley*.

2 CARGOES

28 Coal was the principle cargo of the canals, from the first cargoes from the Duke of Bridgewater mines in 1761, to the last regular long haul traffic on the canals, which came to an end in 1970 with the cessation of carrying by Blue Line. One of the specialist coal carriers were Samuel Barlow Coal Co Ltd, who were one of the last to trade. They too expanded in the 1930s to boast a fleet of 100 boats, several of which were made by the famous Nurser Boat Yard, at Braunston, which Barlows subsequently took over in 1941. Barlows were very aware of competition from other forms of transport and so they took over a number of canal carrying firms and owner-boatmen who had good coal contracts, and they also started a fleet of their own lorries. In 1962 the last few pairs of Barlow boats were sold, along with the Braunston base, to Michael Streat of Blue Line Cruisers, who continued to allow his few pairs to trade until 1970. Here, a Samuel Barlow Coal Co Ltd motorboat fully laden is seen towing two butties. The date is thought to have been early in the 1950s. The towing of two butties is unusual and it can only be assumed that they were on short haul traffic on a relatively lock-free stretch of canal, possibly supplying Coventry Power Station from the nearby Warwickshire Coalfield.

29 This is the Samuel Barlow butty *Little Marvel* purchased by Barlows in June 1941 from David Hambridge, along with motorboat *Fair Trader*. The boat is fully laden with little freeboard, and is complete with slack boards enabling a higher load to be carried at the stern. The bicycle on the coal is for lock wheeling (sending a member of crew ahead to set the locks). The stands are only at half height with the top planks laid along them. Note the dog and its kennel amidships. A very stout boat shaft is also to be seen on top of the cargo — a very essential piece of the boat's equipment.

30 The boats from the Anderton Company were mainly used to carry the products required by the pottery industry up from Weston Point Docks to Stoke-on-Trent and the Five Towns. While many of them managed to get return cargoes of finished pottery products, some returned empty or had to look for other cargoes. Here a pair of Anderton boats wait near the southern entrance of the Harecastle Tunnel at Chatterley, loaded with coal which they have loaded in or around Stoke-on-Trent, and which they will be delivering to the salt industry around Middlewich. This photograph was taken by the late Tom Rolt on the 28 September 1948. The repairs which have been carried out to the bridge abutments were caused by mining subsidence; the same problem has caused much trouble with headroom in the tunnel itself, and in recent years has caused it to be closed altogether for long periods, for rectification.

29

30

31 The principal canal-borne coal to be sold in London was from Warwickshire, and some of the last contracts for supplying coal to the paper mills in Hertfordshire relied on coal from these coal fields. One of the centres in later years for this trade was Hawkesbury Junction where the Northern Oxford Canal met the southern part of the Coventry Canal. Here there was a traffic office where boatmen could go to hear about cargoes of coal — this office would tell them at which pit they could load, and where the destination would be. In the 1960s it was not uncommon to see boats queuing up at Hawkesbury Junction awaiting orders; this picture was taken on a Sunday and there were more boats than loads at that time. These boats belong to British Waterways, Willow Wren Canal Carrying Company, and Samuel Barlow and were photographed in May 1962. Note the pleasure boat threading its way through the moored craft.

32 While coal formed one of the major traffics of the canals, there were many other cargoes carried. The following few photographs illustrate some of them, and others are mentioned throughout the rest of the book. As we have already seen, the factories of the Potteries were some of the last to receive their raw materials by canal, so keeping up the tradition started by Josiah Wedgwood when he instigated the Trent and Mersey Canal in 1765. The raw materials came in at Weston Point docks and finished wares were exported from the same port. Here we see an Anderton Company horseboat *Dudley* at Whatcroft near Northwich in the early 1930s. One of the reasons that the canal could hang onto this traffic was the fact that the return load of finished crockery was very fragile, and water transport has always had the lowest rate of breakages. Most Anderton Company boats had the name of the boat carved into the stern top bend.

33 Roadstone was a regular cargo particularly in the earlier years of trading. Often small wharves were built alongside turnpikes or Parish roads which would only be used for unloading stone for the repair of roads. The County Surveyor of Gloucestershire early this century was quoted as saying 'There are some 70 miles of main road that require some 4,000 tons of roadstone annually for their maintenance. This would all be taken up this canal . . .' The roadstone pictured here was being taken up the Runcorn flight of locks in the 1930s in the motorboat *Elizabeth* and butty *Marjorie* both belonging to Jonathan Horsefield of Runcorn. The butty shows signs of very hard work! Note the timber heads for securing ropes.

34 The firm of Thomas Clayton from Oldbury specialised in the carrying of liquid cargoes. Most of these were the by-products of the gas works, or various grades of oil. In simple terms, these boats were floating tanks. As can be seen from this photograph of the butty *Peel* they are quite low in the water when fully loaded. In this case, the boat is loaded with fuel oil from Stanlow, Ellesmere Port, bound for the Shell-Mex depot at Oldbury, and is proceeding down the Shropshire Union Canal having just passed under Cheswardine Bridge (number 56). The date is March 1955. Because there is no need for the traditional top planks it was no real problem to rig up a washing line to dry the clothes as the boat went along. One of the little girls is holding a doll.

35 A pair of Thomas Clayton boats photographed at High Bridge near Norbury Junction on the Shopshire Union Canal on the 20 April 1955. The motorboat *Tees* was built in 1938. One of the main reasons for Thomas Clayton ceasing carrying was the fact that gas works were closing down. Another important factor which affected the economics of carrying liquids was that it was often virtually impossible to get a return cargo. These boats were carrying oil from the Shell Refinery at Stanlow on the Manchester Ship Canal to Langley Green on the Titford Branch Canal of the Birmingham Canal Navigation. This traffic ceased a few months after this picture was taken. High Bridge is unusual. A number of these high canal bridges are to be found on the Shropshire Union Canal, spanning the very deep cuttings. In this case, the abutments of the bridge have obviously threatened to move, and a strengthening arch has been inserted. Later, with the coming of the telegraph, which for ease of cross-country building was laid alongside roads, railways or canals, a very short telegraph pole was placed on the inner arch to guide the wires around the bridge. At the time of writing, even though the telegraph wires have gone, and most of the poles, this unique one remains.

36

37

36 Cadbury of Bournville is typical of a firm who built their factories beside canals for ease of transport. In 1879 the major chocolate producing plant was moved to Bournville, Birmingham, on the Worcester and Birmingham Canal. They also built milk evaporating factories at Knighton near Market Drayton on the Shropshire Union Canal in 1911, and another at Frampton-on-Severn in 1915, which was adjacent to the Gloucester and Berkeley Ship Canal. Later another factory was built in 1922 at Blackpole near Worcester, again on the Worcester and Birmingham Canal. This picture depicts the old unloading wharf at Bournville. In 1911 they started to run their own fleet of boats carrying various commodities from the docks to the factories, and part-processed materials from one factory to another. Cadbury stopped using their own fleet in 1929, passing most of it over to the Severn and Canal Carrying Co. On nationalisation, British Waterways took over the remnants of the traffic which then ceased in 1961. Between 1966 and 1968 there was a very short revival.

37 One tends to think of canals as carrying only the heavy goods of the industrial revolution, or manufactured products. For many years, Cadburys had a very successful 'milk run' along the Shropshire Union Canal, collecting milk from the farms and taking it to their processing factory at Knighton near Bridge 45. The milk would then be evaporated and added to processed cocoa powder (also brought in by canal as cocoa beans), plus sugar. The resulting product known as 'crumb' was then taken by water to Bournville in Birmingham. Milk boats also operated to Frampton and on a more limited scale to Bournville. The Knighton milk boats were replaced by lorries in 1923. Charles Ballinger's narrowboat *Susan* is dwarfed by the size of this lock at Gloucester. This boat is loaded with chocolate crumb from the Cadbury's milk factory at Frampton-on-Severn, and would be going to Bournville. From Frampton the boat would travel via the Gloucester and Berkeley Ship Canal to Gloucester, then on to the River Severn to Worcester, and then up the fifty-two locks of the Worcester and Birmingham Canal to Bournville. Ballinger was trading on this route up until his death in 1962, when the traffic ceased. This photograph was taken in August 1956. The sheets on this boat still bear the name of the Severn and Canal Carrying Co, and come from two of Ballinger's other boats which were from the fleet of the Severn and Canal Carrying Co.

38 One of the new traffics which developed in the 1930s was that of imported steel from Belgium, coming via the Regents Canal Dock to Birmingham. This is again Sampson Road Wharf and shows *Electra* and *Ethiopia* unloading a cargo of steel bars. It is said that canal carrying was quicker for this cargo than either road or rail by nearly four days, and it cost 2s 7d per ton less. In 1937 the Grand Union Company started its own shipping company, and so brought its own cargoes into London from the continent. The first ship was the steamer *Marsworth* (500 ton cargo capacity) on a weekly service to Antwerp. In 1938 a service to Rotterdam was started using chartered craft. In December 1939 *Blisworth* was acquired and soon after *Kilworth*. Then, in 1945, two new 1,100 ton diesel engined ships *Knebworth* and *Bosworth*. All these ships were sold to the British Transport Commission about 1950 and kept going as an independent fleet.

39 Nobody can say that the Grand Union did not try to get new cargoes. Here in 1938 we see an experimental load of Austin cars, being unloaded at Brentford. They were taken from Brentford to the Austin Showrooms in Oxford Street; presumably it was not thought successful, as it was not repeated. The load was carried in the motorboat *Baldock* and the butty *Lambourne*. In the foreground the dock workers can be seen making up a spreader to attach to the hook on the crane, so that the ropes around the vehicle do not touch the bodywork while it is being craned off. *Baldock* was built by Harland and Wolff and delivered in August 1936; the butty *Lambourne* was built at Rickmansworth and delivered one month earlier.

40 The aim of any canal carrying company would be to keep down the miles covered by their boats when they were empty. Wherever possible back cargoes would be found. In this picture, a group of boats are seen moored at Anderton on the Trent and Mersey Canal on a Sunday morning in the 1930s. These boats are waiting for the Anderton Lift to open on the Monday morning, to enable them to reach the River Weaver and travel to Weston Point docks to collect cargoes of pottery materials for the industries of Stoke-on-Trent. Travelling empty was unprofitable. Down in the south the Grand Union Canal Carrying Co introduced a system of 'boat control', and the positions of all their boats was marked on a large plan. In this way, unnecessary empty mileage could often be avoided.

41

41 A. Harvey-Taylor was a well known carrier in the Aylesbury area, and the lower reaches of the Grand Union Canal. (What a lovely telephone number: 'Phone 9'). Here, however, his boats are not being used for carrying coal, their usual cargo, but people. Before the days of the motor car being generally available, the annual outing of a local church, or some other organisation, really was a 'treat'. Sometimes it took the form of a trip in a trailer behind a traction engine, or, if there was a canal in the area, a journey by canal boat — which had been especially cleaned out for the occasion, fitted with benches or chairs, and, in this case, decked with bunting. Often this was referred to as 'scholar boating'. The date of this outing is thought to be about 1936.

42 This charming study was taken in 1890 and shows an outing on the Kennet and Avon Canal. This is Dundas Wharf, right by the famous Dundas Aquaduct, which is away centre right of the picture. The main line of the canal to Bath goes out under the bridge on the left. Out of the picture, on the extreme right, is the Somersetshire Coal Canal. The boat nearest the wharf is presumably a maintenance craft, looking in poor condition and undecorated, with an old pipe for a tiller. The boat being used for the trip is in much better condition, and like most Kennet and Avon narrowboats is fitted with washboards at the bow for use on esturial waters. The musical trio on the boat complete with harp is a charming touch. The crane on the left is typical of a wharf crane of the time — it was built by Stothert and Pitt of Bath and is still in situ at the time of writing.

3 HORSES AND POWER

43 The simplest way of moving a boat was to haul it by hand, but as we will see from the photographs that follow, animal haulage was much more common. Men were used at first on river navigations where it was necessary to haul boats up through rapids, where there was no real tow path for animal haulage. The River Severn had gangs of men employed in towing the Severn trows up the river. On canals man power was usually reserved for maintenance boats, and only when the boats were required to move short distances, when it was not worth bringing in a horse. Here, around the turn of this century, a maintenance boat is being hauled by two canal workers on the Caldon Canal at Froghall.

44 Animals were used for towing on inland waterways right from the start of the canal age. Horses were the usual choice, though mules and donkeys were not uncommon. The size and type of horse depended on the size of boat being towed, also the width and depth of the waterway. The shire horse was usually reserved for rivers, where large barges had to be towed against the current. Cart horses, van horses and cobs were most common on the Midland canals. Here, on the Grand Union Canal, we see a boat horse accompanied by a member of the boatman's family. Meals for the boat horse had to be taken on the move, hence the horse is eating from a decorated nose bowl.

45 This photograph represents a real working canal horse, with well-worn, but sound, set of harness, coloured bobbins along the flanks to prevent chafing, and a spreader at the rear. The hames have been cut right down to the collar to prevent it catching on the low corners of bridge arches. This horse is blinkered, though this was not universal. The horse is eating from his nose-bowl, but also slung around his neck is a muzzle to prevent the horse being tempted to graze from the hedgerows as he works. With no brakes on the boat, an unscheduled stop by the horse to taste a juicy tuft of grass could cause navigational problems. This picture was taken at Stewponey Lock on the Staffordshire and Worcester Canal in March 1948.

46 Two 'number ones' (owner-boatmen) working up a flight of locks on the Grand Union Canal. The 'number-ones' always owned their horses, and because of this they usually looked after them very well; after all, their very livelihood depended on the fitness of the horse. The larger of the long distance carrying companies usually allocated a horse to a particular boatman, and in this way they could see if it was being looked after properly. In and around Birmingham it was common for the horses to be pooled, particularly by the railway companies, and because of this not so much care was taken of them. The lady on the right is the sister of the late Mrs Arthur Bray, one of the last boatwomen working for Blue Line in 1970.

45

46

47 In some cases, pairs of donkeys were preferred, and these could be seen on some of the canals leading down to the River Severn, the Stroudwater Navigation, the Worcester and Birmingham and the Droitwich. This delightful photograph, taken by de Salis in 1895, shows a boatman's son posing with one of a pair of donkeys on the Worcester and Birmingham Canal at Cobbets Bridge. Donkeys were always known as 'animals' by the boatmen. It can be clearly seen that the harness on these donkeys are not really as elaborate as on some boat horses. In particular, tatty knotted rope replaces the usual side rope with bobbins, and the collar looks well worn. Boatmen in particular would try and keep the collar of the harness dry, because if it got wet, it was liable to chafe and cause serious sores. While one often sees boatmen in old photographs dressed in their Sunday best, this is far more typical — old worn-out coat and trousers, serving as a rain-coat as well as for warmth.

48 The boat horse was seldom allowed to walk on its own; it usually had the boatman ('backer') or more commonly one of his children walking behind, or in some cases actually riding on its back! The presence of someone with the horse kept it on the move, kept the tow rope taut, and in particular stopped the horse from trying to graze from the hedgerows. It was important that the tow paths were kept in good order, so that the horse could obtain maximum grip — in winter a muddy tow path could be a nightmare. Henry de Salis writing in his *Canals and Navigable Rivers* in 1904, comments on how bad tow paths were in some places: 'In winter nothing but a slough of mire, and bounded by a hedge so overgrown as seriously to curtail the width necessary for the passage of the horse.' In this charming picture taken by de Salis in 1895 on the Worcester and Birmingham Canal the hedge is in good order, but bank protection has been neglected.

49 The blacksmith was a very important man for the owner of a horse-drawn boat. Where there was a lot of stop/start work, such as on the Birmingham navigations a horse needed shoeing every two weeks, a little less often on long haul work. Because of the strain on the horses feet, particularly when starting a boat from rest, they were fitted with a shoe which had a clip on it which gripped the toe of the hoof. Special projections called calkins were forged onto the shoe, like spikes on a pair of running shoes, to give more grip on the tow path. In this picture, dated 1922, H. Beck, blacksmith to the Oxford Canal Company is shoeing a horse owned by the canal company. The horse was purchased as a three-year-old from a Mr S. Strong for £40.

50 It was particularly important that the canal horse had stabling overnight. Again the boatman had to look after his horse, and he could not afford it to catch a chill. Canal companies provided stables at various points along the waterway, which usually could be used by the fleet owners or 'number-ones', as well as the company horses, on payment of a fee. A notice at Audlem on an old stable there still proclaims that the stables could only used 'by the canal company's horses'. Waterside pubs often had stables attached. In this photograph, two boat children have harnessed up the horses for the morning start. The location is somewhere on the Grand Union Canal. Maintenance on the building seems to have been sadly neglected.

49

50

51 Narrowboats were not designed to sail, and very few of them did. However, boats working out of the Chesterfield Canal on the River Trent regularly rigged a sail when on the open river. In this photograph we see a pair of narrowboats permanently fitted out with a mast set in a latchet along with the appropriate rollers for halliards to raise and lower the square sail. The inside narrowboat is interesting, as it has no cabin showing. *Rose* on the left is a typical lower Trent keel. It is very unusual to see a narrowboat with a dinghy (coggie boat) in tow, but presumably this was because of the river voyage.

51

52

52 The first mechanisation of the narrowboat came in 1864 when the Grand Junction Co used *Dart* for their London to Braunston run. *Dart* was a steamer. Gradually the steamer became more and more efficient, but its predominant problem was the fact that the engine and boiler took up ten tons of cargo space. Fellows Morton & Clayton were the principal users. Here we see one of their steamers waiting at Rickmansworth Lock with its tow, an ex-horse butty *Boxmoor*. The steersman on the butty is using his tillerbar as a boat shaft to push the boat across the cut, to enable two horsedrawn boats going the other way to pass. As the horse passes under the bridge, so the tow line will rub the brickwork, here protected by a metal upright. The continual rubbing by the ropes has caused the metal to be worn away to produce the serrated edge we see here.

53 On most steamers, the fuel burned was coke, because it was virtually smokeless, but on the Grand Union Canal Charles Nelson of Stockton had three steamers which burned coal, and were normally very smokey, on a regular cement run. Fumes from steamers caused a tragedy in Blisworth tunnel when two crew members were overcome and killed. It was the smooth power of the steamers which made them popular, and they could tow a number of butties if required. The steamer died out in the earlier part of this century, as the motor boat gradually came in. The last recorded steam boat was Fellows Morton & Clayton's *Earl*, which finally came out of service in 1931. Here we see a loaded Fellows Morton & Clayton steamer with butty, southbound for City Road Basin, London, passing under some bridge repairs at Little Woolstone Bridge, in May 1905.

54 One of the problems with steamers was that they required a crew of at least three, and usually four. What with this and the smaller cargo space, they were not an economical proposition unless they were used to run 'fly'; this means that they ran virtually non-stop from the start of the trip to the finish, often carrying perishable cargoes which could not be delayed. Here we see the crew of a Fellows Morton & Clayton steamer posing while the boat is travelling at full speed. In the foreground are the steam whistle and the chimney from the steam plant. Behind are a box-like structure over the engine room serving as a form of skylight, and a chimney from the cabin stove. The date is thought to be about 1900. Avril Landsell in her book *Clothes of the Cut* tells us that Fellows Morton & Clayton issued a type of uniform to their steam boat crews: '. . . they had jackets, too, also with velvet collars, and flat caps. While the jackets were often discarded, the caps were worn even on the hottest days.'

55

56

similar engine *Dickie* were built in 1876 for internal use at Crewe works, both were 0-4-0 tanks. The experiment was not successful and was not tried again. One of the main problems was keeping the leading boats away from the bank — note the crew members with long boat shafts. Such a system could only have been planned for stretches of canal which had a regular short haul traffic. Obviously the engine would have to take the place of the horse altogether, otherwise it would have no point. It is thought that up to eight boats could be pulled by this locomotive, and a speed of seven miles per hour has been reported. In later years barge towing by tractor was commonplace on the lower Grand Union, the Regents Canal and Lee Navigation, and here special precautions in the form of a quick release pedal had to be used in the event of the barge over-running the tractor as it could easily pull it into the canal.

57 Fellows Morton & Clayton were one of the first carriers to successfully use the single cylinder semi-diesel engine made by the Swedish firm of Bolinder. These were the first really successful internal combustion engines to be used on the canals. They fitted their first Bolinger engine in 1912 and remained loyal to that firm until they ceased carrying. In this photograph, taken in 1930 at Barnton on the Trent and Mersey, two Fellows Morton & Clayton motorboats are being used to tow some butties — an unusual sight. Back in 1911 there had also been an experiment powering a boat with a Brooke paraffin engine. It was reported as being very successful, though nothing more was heard of it. Brooke, a Lowestoft firm better known for their cars at that time, later concentrated on marine engines. Various other experiments were tried with different types of propulsion in the earlier years of this century. John I. Thornycroft of Chiswick fitted a 30hp gas motor to the boat *Duchess* in 1906, while in 1908 Crossleys built a suction gas engine for *Vulcan*. Electric power and water jet propulsion was also tried. One of the experiments consisted of a petrol engine, the 'Hook Detachable Motor', mounted on the cabin roof which drove an outboard propellor over the stern. It was heavy to steer and proved unpopular with the crews. There were also problems with clearance under bridges when the boat was running light and was high out of the water. The steersman's vision was also impeded. This experiment was carried out during the latter years of World War I.

55 *Speedwell* was originally built in 1884 and came to Fellows Morton & Clayton via William Clayton in 1889. She was completely rebuilt by Fellows Morton & Clayton in their dock at Saltley in March 1894. This picture of her tied up at Braunston in 1923 was taken two years before she was scrapped. While a boatwoman and children are shown on the cabin roof of the steamer, it was very unusual for these to be family boats. On a few occasions at the end of World War I, a husband and wife partnership ran a steamer, usually with help, but this was unusual. The crew normally consisted of three or four men.

56 An unusual form of motive power for towing narrowboats was experimented with in 1888 on the Middlewich branch of the Shropshire Union Canal, a waterway controlled by the London and North-Western Railway. Near Worleston almost a mile of 18in gauge railway track was laid along the towpath of a straight piece of canal. This was the idea of Francis W. Webb, the mechanical engineer from the LNWR's Crewe works, who is seen standing out front on the left. The name of this diminutive locomotive is thought to be *Billy;* it had the advantage of being able to be driven from either end. *Billy* and another

58

59

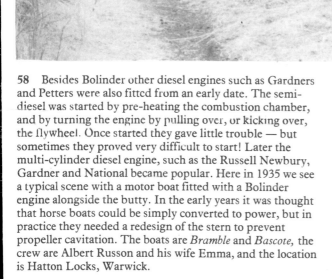

58 Besides Bolinder other diesel engines such as Gardners and Petters were also fitted from an early date. The semi-diesel was started by pre-heating the combustion chamber, and by turning the engine by pulling over, or kicking over, the flywheel. Once started they gave little trouble — but sometimes they proved very difficult to start! Later the multi-cylinder diesel engine, such as the Russell Newbury, Gardner and National became popular. Here in 1935 we see a typical scene with a motor boat fitted with a Bolinder engine alongside the butty. In the early years it was thought that horse boats could be simply converted to power, but in practice they needed a redesign of the stern to prevent propeller cavitation. The boats are *Bramble* and *Bascote,* the crew are Albert Russon and his wife Emma, and the location is Hatton Locks, Warwick.

59 With the coming of the motorboat, the hull design of the boat had to be altered to suit. The rear counter had to be altered to make sure that the propeller was always getting maximum grip on the water and not suffering from cavitation, whereby the propeller creates a 'hole' in the water, so loosing grip. The water must be made to flow evenly over the propeller and correct hull design is the way to achieve this. It is also necessary to see that the water passes evenly past the rudder so that the boat can be steered easily and accurately. In this picture of Mersey Weaver motorboat *Eileen* taken in the 1930s near Barnton a lot of water disturbance can be seen around the stern. This is caused mainly by the shallowing of the canal under the

bridge and the effect of the constriction within the bridge hole. The design of the propeller should also take that into account as well as being designed for maximum thrust forwards. It must also be effective in reverse for braking.

60 Two of the last boats to be built by the British Waterways Board at the yard of E. C. Jones of Brentford in 1960/61 were the motorboats *Anne* and *Lee.* Both were fitted with an extraordinary detachable Harbormaster power/drive unit and they were also wheel steered. With hindsight, it seems strange that such an unconventional device should have been seriously considered so late in the development of the narrowboat. These boats were not a success and they were used mainly on the short haul work such as the 'lime juice run' on the lower Grand Union. In this picture *Anne* with butty *Beryl* are moored above Hatton top lock on one of their rare trips to Birmingham; possibly a test trip. In theory the motor was said to be detachable. The boats were also designed with a detachable cabin and the lifting tackle can be seen bolted to the sides of the cabin of *Anne. Beryl* does not seem to be fitted with a cabin at all! Apart from the novel motor and cabin the boats had a completely new design and new arrangement for covering the holds. This was a series of blue fibreglass hoops over the cargo, which gave the boats the nickname 'bluetop'. When British Waterways Board ceased their carrying activities in 1963 both motorboats and some butties were sold

4 TECHNIQUES OF BOATING

61 The Grand Union Canal was one of those waterways which was both wide and deep enough for a good horse to pull two boats. Clearly shown in this photograph are the boat's running blocks along the top planks. Through these holes runs the tow line from the pulley block in the mast head. The 'snubber' (towing rope) is then fixed to a stud immediately in front of the steersman. This photograph taken on 29 July 1928 shows boats north-bound in Cassiobury Park, Watford, approaching Iron Bridge Lock. It shows how the banks of the canal have been allowed to be eroded, though the towing path itself is still in quite good order. Under the management of the Grand Union Canal Co much dredging and piling took place. The leading boat of this pair is called *James*. The second boat *Verbena* is, happily, still with us, having been completely restored by M. E. Braine in 1974, and belongs to the Cheddleton Flint Mill Industrial Heritage Trust. The craft is exhibited at Cheddleton on the Caldon Canal under the name *Vienna,* the name she received on launching at Saltley Dock in 1911. She was given the new name *Verbena* four years later.

62 Here, the stud in the cabin top is clearly visible with the tow rope running to it. In this case the Samuel Barlow butty *John* is about to leave Stoke Hammond Lock on the Grand Union Canal, and the tow has not been taken up, hence the slack rope. By having the rope fixing point immediately to hand the steersman had full control over the distance between himself and the boat or horse in front. This was helpful when rounding sharp bends, or if it became necessary to cast off in a hurry. If the boat was travelling on a river it was desirable to vary the tow line length as the river wound about. It was easier for the horse if the steerer paid

out or took in the line as the distance between the horse and the boat varied on bends. It is clear from this photograph that the stud is removable otherwise it would foul the cabin slide which normally covered the way down into the cabin. Clearly shown in the picture is the tunnel hook just below the castle painting. This hook was used when boats were breasted up (lashed side-to-side), or when mooring. Also when being towed in a train through a tunnel by a tug, a 'V' rope bridle leading from each tunnel hook would divide the tow rope to avoid fouling and damaging the rudder. The steerer is Bill Humphries.

63 When working the wide Grand Union Canal with its locks which would take two boats side by side, towing between the locks was usually undertaken on a short line, known as a 'snatcher' or 'short strap'. One of the problems with this method was steering the butty, because of interference with the flow of water caused by the propeller of the motor boat. This is the reason for the butty being placed to one side in this picture. When travelling on the open canal, the boats would be separated by a line giving some 60ft between them. This line usually ran from the towing mast and not the bow stud. The photograph was taken in Cassiobury Park, Watford on 29 May 1956. The motorboat was British Waterways *Gardenia* steered by J. Beechey; the butty was called *Meteor*. The strange structure behind the butty is a bridge carrying the towpath over an overflow weir leading to the River Grade.

64

65

64 A pair of British Waterways narrowboats leaves Fishery Lock at Boxmoor on the Grand Union Canal. The steersman on the motorboat is re-fixing the short 'snatcher' to the forepin of the butty. The date was 24 June 1956. The small wheel just inside the cabin on the motorboat controls the throttle. The fenders at the stern of the motorboat are clearly shown; these were a banana shaped 'tip cat' fender, plus a circular one on top, the main purpose of which was to protect the projecting rudder from damage, either from a towed butty or from the chance of the boat being thrown back on to a lock gate.

65 On certain waterways pairs of boats were often towed by a very short crossed strap and the bow of the butty was pulled up tight onto the stern fender of the motorboat. This tended to give the effect of an articulated lorry, and the butty required only minimal steering. It was unusual to see two boats being towed in this way, as in this photograph of a Samuel Barlow motorboat and butties travelling empty in the vicinity of the Warwickshire coalfields.

66 When empty boats travelled on a wider waterway, such as the Grand Union Canal, which was heavily locked, they were often tied together side by side. This was known as 'breasting up'. When loaded, boats were not breasted up, as they became cumbersome to handle and difficult to steer. When a pair of boats were travelling breasted up, it was normal to lock the steering on one. Usually if it was a motor with a butty the tiller of the butty would be centred and held by means of a light rope from each cabin side. In this photograph, taken in 1910, two horse-drawn boats, towed by a single horse, are leaving lock 55, Berkhampstead. In this case a light rope has been stretched from tiller to tiller, and there is also one from the top of each rudder. These holes are also used to fix a rudder check line. Once in a lock, it is often necessary to pull the rudder hard over to clear the gates — this means removing the tiller to avoid fouling the lock sides — hence the use of a check line. The boats are *John* and *Joseph* from the fleet of Joseph Arnold of Camden Town and Leighton Buzzard. They specialised in taking sand to the London area.

67 This pair of narrowboats seen at Clegg Hall, Littleborough on the Rochdale Canal, has been breasted up with the boats facing in opposite directions. When previously published, the author said he did not know why; Mr Maddock, a life long worker on the Trent and Mersey Canal wrote and gave the following explanation: 'When two boats were breasted up like this, only one set of steering gear was needed, because both craft would move together . . . when they reached their destinations they could be steered back to their starting place simply by using the other boat's tiller, so obviating the need to turn them round.' Rather the same idea as having controls at both ends of a tram car! This was presumably a northern habit as the author has never seen reference to it in the south.

68 Bringing a pair of boats into a wide lock was a tricky problem. In this case, two horse-drawn boats came into lock 53 at Berkhampstead on the Grand Union Canal, about 1906. The first boat has come in, while the second is slowly drifting in. Should the forward progress be too fast, the crew member would take a turn of the fore strap around the bollard, so 'strapping' the boat to a stand-still. The bollard on the left has had plenty of this treatment. Already one of the gates at the tail of the lock is being closed, while the boatman has his windlass poised on the paddles of the bottom gate to open them as soon as he can. It can also be seen that the lock keeper has a little allotment at one side of the lock.

69 Bringing a motorised pair of boats into a wide lock had similar problems. Here we see the motorboat has entered first and is gliding in along the lock side, having cast off the tow rope to the butty. The butty, moving under its own impetus, is steered for the gap between the stern of the motorboat and the opposite lock-side. Should the butty be thought to be going too quickly, it can be steered to rub alongside the motorboat and so take off some of the way. This is a lock on the Grand Union Canal and the boats are from the Warwickshire Canal Carrying Co from Charity Dock at Bedworth. The small hut would have been used by the canal lengthsman. The large fender on the stem of the motorboat was obligatory to stop damage to lock gates.

70 Because, of course, time was worth money, the boatmen were always looking for ways in which they could cut corners and speed up their progress. If they could speed up the operation of locks this was of great help to them. When travelling downhill a line could be passed around a hand rail and when it was time for the gate to be opened the motor would go into reverse and pull the gates towards it. As the boat passed out of the lock, the line, which had been affixed by a special knot, would drop away. The boatmen had to allow for the drop in the level of water. In view of the varying drops it must have required some practice to get it right! Here a pair of British Waterways boats emerge from one of the Bascote Locks on the Grand Union. The butty steerer can be seen retrieving the line from the rail of the left-hand gate, the boats having opened the lock gates with a line. This photograph, taken early in 1969, shows the last British Waterways boats trading on the cement run from Kaye's Arm, Long Itchington, to Sampson Road, Birmingham. The boats are *Banstead* and *Tow*. The traffic finished at Easter 1969.

71 This is Iron Bridge Lock, Watford, and the boatman in charge of the motorboat is deliberately sending a stream of water from the propellor in the direction of the opened lock gate, the idea being to get enough force of water behind the gate to start it closing. At the same time the lad (note his bicycle) is opening the paddles at the far end of the lock. The force of the water coming into the lock, will complete the closing operation of the bottom gate. The two ground paddles at the far end will be opened first. Later, when the water has risen sufficiently, the paddles on the gates themselves will be drawn. This must be done with caution to avoid flooding the fore-end of the boat. This picture was taken on 19 June 1937.

72 A pair of boats leave Iron Bridge Lock in the earlier days of nationalisation. In order to save time when leaving the lock, only one top gate has been opened, both boats leaving by the same side. On the right of the lock can be seen the ridged walkway which has been strategically placed to give maximum grip to the crew when opening or shutting the lock gate. Iron Bridge Lock is in Cassiobury Park, Watford, and being a very attractive area, it is frequently photographed. It was one of the primary conditions of building that the canal in this area that it had to blend into the parkland.

73

73 . The techniques of working a narrow lock are of course different. This is lock 6 of the Stockton flight on the Grand Union Canal in Warwickshire. The motorboat has entered the lock, and cast off the tow; the butty is losing speed but will eventually end up nudging the closed top gate of the lock or the neighbouring lock surround. This is an unusual picture as it shows the narrow locks still being used after the wide locks (on the right) were built. These wide locks were part of the Grand Union's modernisation schemes of the 1930s. Soon after this photograph was taken the single locks were abandoned, the bottom gates were replaced by brick walls which acted as overflow weirs. In this case the wide lock is stanked off for repair. The butty is the Grand Union Canal Company's boat *Ayr* and if normal practice was being followed, the motorboat was *Aynho,* both built in 1936. The buildings with the chimneys on the left of the canal were lime works.

74   One of the reasons why narrowboats were built to take hard knocks was the fact that they had no brakes and sometimes had to rely on running into things or alongside the bank, to finally bring them to a standstill. E. Temple Thurston on his trip with Eynsham Harry and his boat the *Flower of Gloster* about 1910 passed through the lock at Cropredy on the Oxford Canal. In the notes which accompany Temple-Thurston's photographs of this trip, in his own photograph album which is happily still preserved by his widow, we learn that Eynsham Harry the boatman was '. . . breaking the pace of the barge with gate on the entrance to the lock . . ." This was certainly one way which boatmen used to slow down the boats.

75 A pair of narrowboats working through Audlem Locks on the Shropshire Union Canal in the twilight of commercial carrying. Admiral Class motorboat *Mountbatten* and butty *Keppel* operated by the Anderton Canal Carrying Co were returning from Wolverhampton where they had delivered a load of piles for a canalside pipe line project on 19 February 1971. The motorboat has proceeded through the lock and would have normally gone on to the next lock leaving the person in charge of the butty to man-handle the butty into the lock. In this case the boatman's wife has gone shopping in Audlem and the boatman is hauling the butty in by hand. Shopping had to be undertaken very swiftly while the boats were travelling, although more time could be spared when they were tied up at the end of the journey.

76 Climbing a flight of narrow locks, particularly if equally spaced as on the Shropshire Union Canal, can be speeded up if the technique of 'long lining' is used. Here the motorboat locks through, and once the lock has been emptied again the butty is towed in by the motorboat, the line running from the stern of the motor to the highest point on the butty — the towing mast. The line of course has to run over the top gate of the lock. The long line was usually a couple of towing ropes joined together. It has been suggested that long lining would only work going uphill and not downhill. This photograph on the Adderley flight of the Shropshire Union Canal proves that long lining can work downhill. The motorboat *Avis* is in lock 4, whilst the butty *Jesmond* is in lock 3 of the flight. The pair are carrying a load

75

of pipes and the date is 20 April 1957. The marks at the end of the lock balance beam have been caused by boatmen closing the gates when locking downhill with the aid of the pointed boat shaft. The canal company has provided a special pad on the gate, so that the beam itself does not suffer.

76

77

78

77 It was once common practice, standard to all boatmen, not to close the gates of a lock as they left it. Here a pair of Thomas Clayton tarboats leave the top lock of the Audlem flight on the Shropshire Union Canal. No attempt is being made to shut the top gate, nor close the paddle on the non-towpath side. There was always a 50/50 chance that the next boat would be coming in the opposite direction, so saving them a little time. Had a boat been following no doubt they would have sent someone ahead to close the lock gates after this boat had left. Nowadays, British Waterways ask all boaters to close all gates and paddles behind them to conserve water supplies in the event of leakage. The motorboat is *Usk,* captained by Ben Smith, and built at Uxbridge in 1939. The butty is called *Mole* and was built by Nursers of Braunston in May 1932, and crewed by Jack Taylor. It looks as if the pair are being worked by two couples and in this photograph the men are on the motorboat and the women on the butty.

78 This photograph will give the reader some idea of the size of rudder or helm on a towed butty or a horse boat. This newly docked boat is running empty with a large part of the rudder out of the water, though there still would be about one foot below water level. The rudder is very substantially built and very heavy, and to give the maximum of manoeverability it has a very long tiller fixed to it. The tiller can be seen here swung fully over the projecting a long way outside the boat. The top part of the rudder into which the

tiller fits is called the ram's head and is usually highly decorated with a variety of ropework designs on it to protect the paint. Sometimes a horse's tail was hung down from the top of the ram's head. This scene is the approach to the top lock at Audlem on the Shropshire Union Canal, and the steerswoman is trying to slow down the butty — remember narrowboats had no brakes — even motorboats find stopping difficult! The boats are from British Waterways north-western fleet.

79 Again we can see the full stretch of the rudder and tiller and it can be appreciated why they had to be this size. To gain a better purchase on the water, the steersman even tries rowing the stern around with the rudder, as seen here, moving it quickly backwards and forwards. Even with all this effort it can be seen that the butty is almost certain to hit the bank — boats were built for this sort of treatment, as were the banks on such corners. The strength required for constant steering of a loaded butty can be imagined. This picture, taken in September 1954, at Gayton Bridge No 2, shows a pair of British Waterways boats on the Northampton Arm of the Grand Union Canal bound for the mills at Wellingborough. The wooden butty is the ex-Grand Union Canal Carrying Co's *Hadfield,* built by Walkers of Rickmansworth in May 1938.

80

81

80 Dredging is a very important part of canal maintenance (see later chapter). Only if there is sufficient depth of water can full cargoes be carried. Here a pair of Samuel Barlow coal boats are 'stemmed up' on the Oxford Canal. The motorboat has been stopped by grounding and then hit by the butty, which has slewed across the canal. In many cases it is only possible to get the boats away from grounded situations such as this by getting the stern of the motorboat (the part of the boat with the deepest draught) out into the channel and pulling the boat off in reverse. Once the boat is in deep water it should be possible to tow the butty off the obstacle. The motor *Admiral* and the butty *Mosquito* were taking 44 tons of ⅜in nuts from Griff Colliery on the Coventry Canal to the Co-op coal yard at Banbury in July 1955. Note the slack boards enabling the butty to carry more coal.

81 A pair of British Waterways boats going south on the Grand Union Canal near Bugbrooke with a cargo of coal. While the side cloths have not been put up, nor have the top planks been erected, the cratch is in position and covered with a tarpaulin and is complete with its circular whorls of ropework. The cratch is a triangular structure facing forward at the bow, which protects the front of the cargo and provides a support for the top planks. It was usually found on Midland and Southern boats, but not often in the north. Many Grand Union Canal Carrying Co craft fitted a false

cratch behind, giving a covered area at the fore end of the boat. Such a structure is seen here. On the butty, the washing line has been hung from the towing mast to a post just forward of the cabin. One item of maintenance which was often neglected were trees and branches over-hanging the canal. These could remove the washing, or any other loose items such as water cans, or ropes which may have been on the cabin roof.

82 This undated painting captures, almost more than any photograph, the typical conditions under which the canal boatmen and women had to work. Here in an industrial area the horse has had to be unhitched because of the lack of tow path, and the boat is being manoevered by a boatwoman with the aid of the long shaft. Normally a horse-drawn narrowboat carried two or three shafts, as there were many occasions when an unpowered boat had to be moved manually. Shafts are very useful for bringing a boat sideways into the bank, or for poling it off the mud. The shafts carried would include a short cabin shaft kept handy on the cabin roof, usually with the business end nearest to the steerer as this was the easiest way to grip it in a hurry. The young woman steering the boat also appears to be clutching a young baby, again giving some indication of how family life continued under these trying working conditions.

83

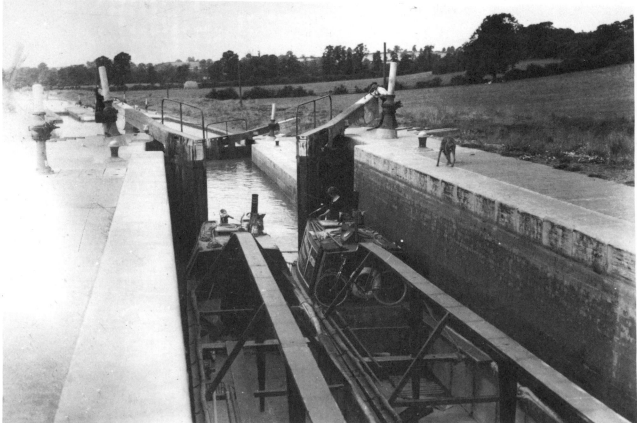

84

83 Anyone who has tried to moor a narrowboat by the side of the Ashby Canal (and many others) will know that the banks usually shelve very gradually towards the centre of the waterway. It is often impossible to moor alongside the bank, and part of this problem is due to poor dredging. The coming of the motorboat, with its excessive wash, broke down the banks, slowly filling up the canal. This is Shardlow on the Trent and Mersey Canal in 1949 and a pair of Fellows Morton & Clayton boats are unable to moor close to the bank. They are close in at the stern, but the fore end is quite a way out. When moored, the steersman on the butty will remove the tiller from the rudder and turn it round so that it points upwards to give good headroom for access in and out of the cabin. The motorboat was built by Fellows Morton & Clayton at Uxbridge in 1919, and is called *Rover*. The butty *Grace* was built at Uxbridge in April 1929. Shardlow was an inland canal port, where the canal met the River Trent. While pleasure cruising on the canals is mainly a post-World War II phenomenon, river crusing has been popular for much longer, hence the cabin cruiser in the background.

84 Once a cargo had been unloaded it was often necessary for the hold to be meticulously cleaned in order to accept the next cargo, which could be quite a different type of load. It was particularly important that when carrying grain the holds were very clean, and then were lined with white sheets. Here a pair of empty Grand Union Carrying Co boats ascend the double lock on the Bascote Flight on their way from Birmingham to Braunston. Inside the empty holds are a variety of shafts, boat hooks and weed rakes. The stretching chains across the hold on both boats are clearly seen in the foreground, and these prevent the sides of the boat spreading when fully loaded. These chains can be tightened by a buckle screw and are complimentary to beams and stretchers which prevent sides being forced inwards if the boat was heavily laden in the bottom. On the right is the motorboat *Arcturus* and on the left the butty, most probably the *Sirius*.

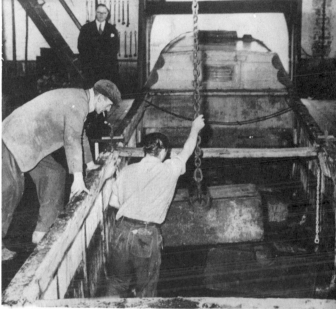

85 For most of the years when commercial traffic travelled on the canals the boatmen paid tolls to the canal companies, in exactly the same way as the tolls used on turnpikes and roads. Tolls were levied on the basis of the weight that was being carried and the type of cargo. Each toll office would have a set of tables, setting out the displacement of each boat when carrying various weights of cargo. The boat would be 'gauged' to find the amount of freeboard, from which the actual weight being carried can be calculated. It was not always possible to undertake the gauging from the bank, as in this picture, which shows a pair of Fellows Morton & Clayton boats being gauged. The toll clerk is standing on the counter of the motorboat while measuring the butty. The toll clerk would issue the boatman with a ticket or receipt, but would usually expect to be paid in cash. The boatman would normally have a small drawer under the roof of the cabin on the left-hand side, which was known as the ticket drawer in which his tolls for a trip would be kept. All the major carriers, such as Fellows Morton & Clayton, had toll accounts. The motorboat is *Lapwing*, and the butty *Kilburn*.

86 In order to obtain an accurate measurement of the displacement of a boat it had to be loaded with a known weight of cargo. A number of weighing stations, or weigh docks, existed around the country and this is the one at Tipton, near Birmingham, beside the top lock of Factory Locks. Usually the cargo for weighing purposes were half-ton or one-ton metal weights, which were loaded into the boat one at a time and the displacement noted. Stone weights were used at first, but these were gradually worn undersize by abrasion. In May 1963 British Waterways changed its sytem of charging, doing away with tolls on many waterways and substituting an annual licence instead. Tolls still had to be paid on commercial waterways by carrying craft, but on cruising waterways working boats pay an annual licence, as do pleasure craft. This picture was taken during the latter days of gauging, in 1958, when this gauging station was only in use on the first Wednesday of each month. This must have been one of the last boats to be gauged.

87 Work had to go on, even if it was raining. Some boatmen rigged up temporary shelters around the steering position on their boats to protect them from the elements. Mr and Mrs Harry Bently seen here in pouring rain in December 1956 seem to have fixed up very crude weather protection. It is surprising that the butty steerer can see anything at all. This is a Runcorn type narrowboat. The photograph was taken on the Bridgewater Canal when the boats were carrying coal from the pits near Leigh to the gasworks at Runcorn. It is interesting to note that the motorboat has a modified counter due to the fact that it has been converted from a horse-drawn boat. A counter has been built out from the original, and ballasted with concrete. In this case it has been possible to keep the horse boat helm. *Winifred* was owned by Jonathan Horsefield of Canal Street, Runcorn.

88 Serious accidents to narrowboats were rare, but they did sometimes happen. One such accident occurred in October 1913; the butty *Buckingham* was being towed north by a steamer. Near Stoke Hammond the butty got too close to the bank on a bend, and started to keel over; almost immediately the cargo of coils of wire rope shifted, causing the butty to turn over on its side. Normally, of course, narrowboat cargoes were not securely fixed in the hold as it was never expected that the boats would get themselves into a position where they would be leaning over. Here a horse-drawn boat navigates past the stricken craft. The boat on the right is some form of maintenance craft, no doubt brought in to help with the salvage operation.

89 Accidents can also happen in controlled conditions. In May 1910 the horse-drawn boats *India* and *Stockport* were both in the weigh dock at Brentford. While the weights were being loaded into *Stockport* from the overhead crane, those in the hold somehow shifted, and the boat tipped on to its side. The poor unfortunate families were then photographed by the local photographer, and the subsequent picture issued as a postcard. Later the dock was drained, the weights taken out of the hold one-by-one, and the boat righted. Some of the weights can be seen alongside the dock.

90

91

90 Accidents often caused delay to other boats which of course was very frustrating, and often resulted in the boat owners losing money on the trip. In this case a wide boat *Victory* owned by G. S. Reed, loaded with chalk, had been allowed to catch her stern on the cill of a lock as the water emptied out, so causing her to break her back. It is reputed that the crew were in the nearby pub at the time! The accident has caused a traffic jam with a variety of boats held up, including John Griffiths' of Bedworth *Sarah* on the left. On the right are two more chalk laden boats: W. E. Costin's narrowboat *Rock,* and in front of her a wide boat. The place is Cowley Lock on the Grand Union, and the date was 30 December 1896. Over the lock can be seen erected a tripod; this apparatus known as 'sheerlegs' would have been used to help lift part of the stricken boat to help with the clearance of the obstruction.

91 Like any other transport system, canals need repairs, and in many cases repairs meant closing a section of the waterway and possibly draining it as well. Where there was no alternative route around, this meant delays for trading boats and loss of income. Where possible, routine maintenance took place at weekends or bank holidays, when some boats at least would not be moving. This photograph taken in May 1905 shows boats waiting for the clearance of the annual Whitsun stoppage at the Braunston flight of locks on the Grand Union Canal. In the background is the 2,048yd Braunston Tunnel. The leading pair of boats are a steamer and a butty from the Fellows Morton & Clayton fleet, carrying products from the Bovril factory, hence the advertisement on the cratch of the butty. The steamer has a very tall cratch, a very distinctive feature on some of the Fellows Morton & Clayton boats.

92 For those boats trading regularly in Britain on rivers, flooding was a major hazard. Perhaps the two rivers which were affected the most were the Severn and the Trent. On the Severn tugs were designed especially for towing narrowboats on the river when it was in flood and in this picture, one of them, *Severn Progress* is seen towing a string of boats up-stream past Tewkesbury Abbey and Healings Mill. Journeys of this sort were not without

incident; it only needed a tow rope to break for a boat to be swept downstream and over a weir. In some cases where the boats belonged to 'number-ones' the horses were put on board the boat as well, so as to be available to move the boat at the other end of the tow.

93 Flooding on the canals rarely held up traffic, as it was not often very serious. Drought on the other hand played havoc with schedules. August 1934 was one very bad time. The Grand Union main line was only kept open at the expense of the Leicester Arm, the top 20-mile pound of which was used as a reservoir, and when that was emptied pumps were installed at Foxton to take water up from the Kibworth pound below those locks, which, in turn, was emptied. At the height of the drought, one of the shallowest parts of the main line was the approach to the northern portal of Braunston Tunnel. The low level of the water can be clearly seen in this picture, which shows a pair of boats approaching the tunnel. This motorboat is fitted with a bow cabin, and a beautifully decorative paraffin tunnel lamp at the fore-end.

5 BOAT PEOPLE

women are the blouse and ankle-length skirt with an apron over. Many wore shawls as well as a bonnet. These bonnets with a stiff brim across the front and a 'curtain' hanging over the sholders were common amongst people who spent long hours out in all weather. They changed from light colours to black immediately after Queen Victoria's funeral, and many women continued to wear black up until the 1930s.

94 This illustration first appeared in *The Sphere* on 25 May 1907. Part of the original caption reads as follows: '. . . our canals still present a very old world look with their gorgeously painted boats and queer crews for the merry mariners on our canals remain almost the only people who really wear the "pearly" type of costume formerly associated with the London coster. Whitsun is the season when the bargee appears in all the splendours of new clothes. The picture illustrates the more domestic scenes on board canal boats. . . .' But the caption writer has made a mistake in almost every line! 'Gorgeously painted' is too exotic; possibly highly decorated might be better. 'Queer crews' has a different connotation these days; what the writer means is that he cannot understand the way of life of these people. 'Merry mariners' is not a term normally associated with boatmen. 'Pearly' costume is not normally associated with them either. Did they really buy new clothes for Whitsun?

95 This charming illustration of 1910 is most likely to be far more typical of the working boatman when taking time off. Fellows Morton & Clayton horse boats *Surrey* and *Walnut* are moored together on the Grand Union. The women and children are in their best clothes, while the men appear to be in their working clothes. Typical for the

96 This scene in 1910 is of a neat and tidy, but harrassed-looking Mrs Coles steering her husband's horse-drawn boat. The striped blouse was usual, and the plain apron, while both men and women favoured leather belts. The child in this case is much more plainly dressed. This charming photograph was taken by E. Temple-Thurston when on his trip in the *Flower of Gloster*. The paraphenalia in the foreground on the cabin roof belongs to the photographer, not the boat crew. The large can on the right would have contained drinking water, the only way in which it was normally carried by boatmen. The chimney behind is from the range in the cabin. From the 1920s these chimneys were often decorated by brass rings. In front of the cabin slide is the cabin deadlight which would allow a little light into the cabin when door and slide were shut.

97 In the past, the author has been accused of glamorising the way of life of the boat people, but it is very difficult to glamorise the life of the traditional Midlands boatmen, as portrayed in this picture, taken at Tipton. It was taken around 1905 and shows Charlie Flimpey and family beside their Shropshire Union Railway and Canal Company boat. Though the boat appears to be fully loaded with boxes and barrels they cannot contain much weight, as the boat is still riding high in the water. The dirty appearance of the boating family is much more typical of everyday life than many of the posed groups of photographs which survive. After the Canal Boat Acts of 1877 the minimum amount of air space per person was stipulated for the cabins, which normally meant that

only a husband and wife and two children could live in a back cabin. Some boats were then fitted with a very small fore cabin to take one or two other children. Was Charlie Flimpey breaking the rules, or did he have a pair of boats?

98 and **99** Much has been written about the clothes of the boat families at the turn of this century. Many of the traditional styles continued to be seen as late as World War II. Later, however, general working clothes were more common as seen in the picture of Mr Boswell from the *Greenock,* moored at Stoke Bruerne in 1956, with his collarless shirt, Fairisle type pullover and cardigan. His trousers are of a heavy material, possibly ex-WD. Stout boots are on his feet while a battered trilby covers his head. In wet weather the boatman favoured an overcoat which absorbed the rain and which could then be dried off in the warmth of the engine room. The macintosh was not so popular. In the other photograph, the boatwoman has left her butty in her slippers, to operate Weston Mill Lock on the River Nene. She is wearing a pinafore over her dress, and a cardigan which looks a little small.

100 Though this photograph will be familiar to many readers, it is reproduced again as it surely is the best picture to illustrate what bad weather conditions really meant to the boatmen. Early in the year, there is snow on the ground, and drizzle in the air. The crew are well wrapped up, but look wet through. The lock sides are in poor repair and the ground is very slippery. Can you imagine how the boatmen dry their clothes? This is the Foxton Flight of ten locks, five each in two staircases. On the sky-line another boat is following them down.

101 Families had to be very careful when looking after young children on the boats, as of course it was very easy for them to fall overboard. This photograph was taken during World War II, and shows a boatwoman holding on to her baby, while steering the boat away from Stoke Bruerne, towards Braunston Tunnel. The child is wearing a harness which was often chained to the ring securing the chimney chain, or if the child was in the cabin, to a hook above the side bed. The woman is standing inside the cabin entrance which not only gives her better movement around the tiller, but also gains her warmth from the cabin stove. As in this case, it was common practice for the husband to work the motorboat and leave his wife to steer the butty and look after the children.

102 and **103** Two very contrasting scenes of boat children as they are growing up. The boy with his pet dog very obviously full of mischief has been photographed as the boat is rising in a lock. Presumably he is not considered old enough to help with the working of the boat, though in many cases children younger than this — from the age of three, in fact — would have been seen operating locks or even steering the boat! Sometimes they had to stand on a box if they were not tall enough to see over the cabin roof! The young girl in the other photograph is quite likely far more used to helping her parents with the day-to-day operation of a pair of boats.

104 Living accommodation on a narrowboat has to be kept to a minimum — after all, it takes up valuable cargo space. The average cabin was approximately 10ft long by the width of the inside of the boat, say 6ft 10in. In this area, the boatman had to eat, sleep and rear a family. Here, Mrs Mary Safe is putting up Christmas decorations in December 1956, and the photograph gives some indication of the relatively small amount of room available. The main feature in the rear of the cabin was the range which provided heating and cooking facilities. The bar, or fiddle rail, along the top of it would have stopped saucepans falling off in the event of a bump when the boat was under way. The lamp was the sole means of illumination at night. Besides the decorative lace-edged plates, boatmen collected items made of brass, a number of which can be seen in this photograph. The dipper hanging behind the stove would have been used to obtain water from the canal for washing up and other uses where drinking water was not required. After World War II it was not uncommon to find that boats had a wireless set aboard, and one is seen on the left of this picture. The batteries for the radio were most probably charged from a dynamo on the engine. Above the wireless is a cupboard for cleaning materials, etc.

105 Looking from the stern of the boat, the cabin stove would be on the left, while the main bed would be behind the curtains across the width of the cabin. Here a boatwoman poses, looking after her young baby, which is being cared for in a side bed. The lace-edged plates are typical of the adornment which used to be found in many narrowboat cabins as they were often souvenirs of events, such as coronations or holidays spent at seaside resorts. In this case, they are supplemented by framed family wedding photographs. This picture was taken some time during the early 1940s. Boatmen also made extensive use of chequered linoleum. Many boatmen will tell you they were born in a cabin. When the baby was due, the boat would tie up for a few days. In later years, regulations stated that they had to tie up for twelve weeks, so usually the boatwoman went to stay with relatives 'on the bank' and her husband continued trading.

106 Because of the small amount of space available in the cabin, each piece of furniture had to serve a number of different purposes. The cupboard door for example, would fold down to form a table — it was called a table cupboard. Wood graining, as can be seen here, was a popular form of decoration inside the cabin, along with roses and castles, which do not feature in this particular picture, but were probably on the underside of the table cupboard. As can be imagined, this cupboard would have contained many different items. In this case it is a larder, medicine chest, a cutlery drawer and a piggy bank. The boat people would have to snatch meals wherever they could. They were often up in the morning and away before it was possible to cook a proper breakfast, and on many occasions they would work right the way through the day, snatching snacks whenever this was possible. Usually their main meal would have been in the evening, after they had moored.

107 As we have seen in the introduction to this book the boatmen were a relatively small and tight-knit community, whose origins can only be traced back to the middle of the 1700s. They have, however, developed a very strong folk art which would appear to have become commonplace from the 1830s/1840s onwards, as it does not appear on any of the early engravings by Thomas Shepherd and others. This traditional art features versions of geometrical designs such as clubs, hearts, diamonds and crescent. Versions of the dog rose were the chief floral decoration, along with scenes featuring a castle, a lake with a boat, and a bridge. The principle colours were red, white, blue and green. A fairly typical version is shown here on the famous pair of Samuel Barlow coal boats *Cairo* and *Warwick*. The helm and tiller are highly decorated and the cabin sides besides being sign-written to a very high quality, are also covered with roses. The insides of the cabin doors were always covered with castle scenes on the top panel and roses on the panel below. When the cabin doors were open these showed up, as can be seen in this picture. The anchor symbol by the rudder post is the trade mark of Nurser Brothers yard at Braunston. Not all the ropework on the tiller was decorative, without a purpose. The piece of plaited rope from the stern post up to the rudder pintle was a safeguard in case the rudder ever got lifted out of its sockets.

108 Right from the earliest days of the narrowboat, etchings depict the carrier's name painted on the cabin sides. On horse-drawn boats and butties the name of the boat was usually on the stern top bend or plank. With the coming of the steam powered boat and later the motor with extended cabin sides, the name of the motorboat appeared on the side of the engine room, as with this Fellows Morton & Clayton boat *Buffalo,* built in 1924. Often, as seen here, the design on the inside of the engine room door would match up with the design on the exterior, so completing a panel when the door was opened. This picture, taken on the Trent and Mersey Canal in 1940, shows the steerer standing right inside the cabin, keeping warm, with the cabin doors shut, hence there are no roses and castles facing towards the stern. On motorboats, the tiller was usually decorated in the style of a barber's pole, and had a removable extension, the join of which can be seen in this photograph, just above the swan's neck; note the tiller pin.

109 In general, each boat yard had its own painter, and each painter had his own style. It was usually possible to tell at which yard a boat was last docked by the style of the painting. In this picture taken around 1945, a boatman is decorating a water can. Also in the photograph are a number of striped poles on the cabin tops. These are the handles of the boatman's flannel headed, or 'rag', mops, used for washing down the cabin interiors and exteriors. A number of books and many articles have been written on the origin of these styles of painting, and while they are similar to gipsy art in the Near East, and, more recently, a style of art featured on lorries in Afghanistan, it is very likely that the art form gradually evolved without European mainland influence. There were many art forms existing along the banks of canals both in the form of traditional decorating associated with carrier's carts, as well as with industry. Tony Lewery in his excellent book *Narrowboat Painting* quotes examples of decoration on period furniture, clock faces and in particular the cheap japanning industry. One of the earliest pieces of canal art which is known to survive in its original form is a bread board now in the Black Country Museum dating from 1875, which, while being painted in traditional colours, depicts a horse very much in the style of Stubbs.

110 It is easy to over emphasise the artistic side of the decoration of narrowboats. While some fleet operators were very particular in the way in which their boats were turned out, others really could not care less, as long as their boats actually floated. 'Number-ones' on the other hand, usually had highly decorated boats which they looked after extremely well, often covering the intricate parts of the paint work with a cloth in bright sunlight. By the time of nationalisation in 1948, a lot of the glamour and tradition was disappearing and a new British Waterways style of painting and colours did nothing to help. This photograph is quite likely more typical of the condition of paint work on a working boat than many others in this book, particularly a boat owned by a fleet operator. It is thought the picture was taken at Broad Street Basin, Wolverhampton, in June 1951, which means that the paint work would be no more than three years old, and yet it is in very poor condition. The nearest boat is the butty *Raven* while behind in the distance is the ex-Fellows Morton & Clayton motorboat *Dace*.

111 This photograph was taken in 1948, just before nationalisation. The Grand Union Canal Carrying Company boat *Merak* looks to be well cared for. Unusually, there is a complete lack of decoration on the open cabin doors. The boat family, however, have made quite sure that their water cans are a riot of colour. Two big cans and a dipper, the latter normally used to take water from the canal. It was quite unusual for castles to feature on a can as well as roses. Often the name of the boat or the owner's name was painted on the cans. Nowadays, the holidaymaker on a purpose-built narrowboat has little problem over keeping filled up with water for use by his crew. With the increase in the popularity of pleasure cruising there has also been an increase in the provision of water taps. Most hire boats have a water tank capacity of at least 100 gallons. This not only provides drinking water but also washing water, and in many cases water for a shower as well. Would the working boatman have beeen envious? He carried his sole water supply in these cans on the roof of the cabin. A water tank would have taken up precious room, and the cabin top was a convenient place for the cans to be kept. Also clearly visible in this photograph are the safety chains on the chimney to stop it being swept overboard should it hit an obstruction, and the cabin side strings which would often be used to carry a spare tow line.

112 Many people imagine that the boatmen had a marvellous life travelling all over the country picking up cargoes here and there, and covering great mileages in the process. In practice, although there were several thousand miles of inter-connected navigable waterways to travel upon, most boatmen kept to regular runs, usually over the same canal. 'Number-ones' in particular kept to set patterns of travel. Of all the carrying companics, Fellows Morton & Clayton possibly gave their captains the greatest variety as they had depots and contacts over all the Midland canal system, as well as in Manchester, Liverpool and London. In this picture, taken during the boatmen's strike of 1923, we see a number of Fellows Morton & Clayton crews with their boats at Braunston. The photographer is standing beside the old Braunston narrow stop lock, which was done away with in 1930.

113 ·Pets were popular with canal boatmen's families. By far and away the most popular were dogs, who could not only act as security and as a deterrent but could also catch food. The hedgerows were open to the boatman, his gun and his dog. It is likely that many a rabbit, hare or gamebird has been brought back to the boats by the faithful dog! This dog belongs to Albert Russon who is seen here steering the butty *Bascote* along Denham Straight above Uxbridge Lock. Caged birds were popular at one time too, usually some form of a song bird, and during the day their cages often sat on the cabin tops along with the water cans. Cats too were often found on the boats.

114 Canal boatmen were not known for industrial unrest, and there were very few strikes. Perhaps the best known is the one which took place in 1923 when those boatmen who normally worked the London to Braunston run for Fellows Morton & Clayton went on strike. The strike was over the company's proposal to take away a special bonus awarded to them during World War I. The strike seriously disrupted traffic on the southern part of the Grand Union for seventeen weeks. In this picture, the striking boatmen, their wives and families pose outside the company's dock at Braunston. The gentleman in the trilby hat at the back centre was Mr Brookes of the Transport and General Workers' Union. While the boatmen look peaceful in this photograph, the police were called to the dock to keep order on more than on occasion during the strike.

115 In order to make a reasonable living most canal boatmen had to work six or seven days a week. Any delay or hold up would be used for essential household chores. Here, in 1910, a stoppage at Whilton Locks (now known as Long Buckby) on the Grand Union Canal has given the crews of these Fellows Morton & Clayton boats a chance of catching up with the washing. The water is being boiled on an improvised fire on the tow path, while the boatwomen pound the clothes in the tub with the traditional wooden 'dolly'.

116 Every trading narrowboat had to be registered with a Local Authority, for health inspection purposes. The details of registration were always written on the outside of the cabin, usually along the top of the cabin side above the carrier's name. George Smith, the crusader for the under priviledged amongst the working classes, spent a long time in the 1870s and 1880s campaigning for better living conditions for the boatman and his family. As a result of the Canal Boat Acts of 1877 and 1884 various changes took place which improved their living conditions. Besides outlining how many people could occupy a cabin space, it also stipulated a minimum standard of cabin decor and comfort. Here at Hulme Locks on the Bridgewater Canal, Manchester, in 1951 Frank Lanigan is checking details of registration and making sure all aspects of the Act are being upheld.

118 Boating around Birmingham and the Black Country has been singled out for a separate chapter as the area has a character all of its very own. The area was the heart of British industry, and so required vast quantities of supplies, coal being the most common. Coal was available from the local mines as well as nearby Cannock Chase and other places, and this was transferred by water all over the area. It was mainly short haul work, so most of the boating was day boating, the crews going home each night.

For this reason, some boats had no cabins, or if they were so fitted they were small cabins, which were there only for protection in case of inclement weather, or for use as a mess room. This scene at Hednesford Collieries was taken in 1910. It depicts a very busy wharf with cable hauled trucks of coal having to be tipped on their side for unloading. Note the sheet of metal (with handles) placed over the gap between wharf and boat. The boats were very often neatly stacked, if the cargo was large lumps of coal.

118

117 A pair of boats locking down through the top lock at Stoke Bruerne and up on the lock side the legendary figure of Sister Mary Ward. Sister Mary trained in France but returned in 1934 to the family home by the canal at Stoke Bruerne to look after her father. One patient was not enough, and from 1936 to 1963 she became nurse to the boat people. At first she paid for the work herself, and was about to give up through lack of funds when the Grand Union Canal Company came to the rescue, and paid her a salary. The appointment was continued by British Waterways who retired her in 1960 on a small pernsion. She continued to work from her own resources until 1963, when most of the boats she knew so well were withdrawn. Tim Wilkinson in his book *Hold on a Minute* recalls a conversation with boatman Phelps about Sister Mary 'brought both our kids into the world; looked after Sarah when she had her second miscarriage. Sister Mary is alright. Always wears that long white thing on her head, and you should see her house, so clean and shining a body hardly dares go in. On the walls pictures of bones and all of a man's guts. Quite frightening it is. But she knows everything, and does everything to help the likes of we. She's our nurse, doctor and friend, all in that small body under the white hat. You know she even helps to set the locks, and can wind a paddle, but she says winding paddles is not a woman's work. . . .' Later Sister Mary was honoured with the British Empire Medal, and also had a 'This is Your Life' programme to herself. She died in 1972.

119 In 1850 the Anglesey Branch Canal was built using as a basis the feeder from Cannock Chase Reservoir (Chasewater). The purpose of this canal was to tap the trade from new coal mines being opened up in the area by the Marquess of Anglesey. The basin at the end of the canal was then called Anglesey Basin. In this photograph, thought to have been taken in the 1930s, a variety of Birmingham day boats are seen loading coal under the Cannock Chase Colliery's loading screens. The coal would come down a shute and, as they were being loaded, the boats would be walked backwards and forwards under the shute to make sure they had been loaded evenly.

119

120

121 It was unusual to see a woman on a Birmingham day boat. Possibly as this was a relatively long haul trip for such a boat, the cabin was being used for overnight sleeping. This T. and S. Element boat was photographed at 7.00am in July 1955 about one mile above Curdworth Locks on the Birmingham and Fazeley Canal. Coal was being brought into Birmingham for the GEC plant at Witton from the pits near Atherstone on the Coventry Canal; quite a long trip.

120 One of the firms specialising in moving coal around this area was T. and S. Element Limited of Oldbury, a number of whose boats appear in this photograph. This is a loading dock near Anglesey Wharf, Chasetown. The Wharfinger's office is clearly seen, but the reason for the beehive roofed building next door is not known. It is possibly the shop of a blacksmith, whose chief job would have been the re-shoeing of the many canal horses coming to the wharf. On the Chester Canal near Beeston there are similar huts which were used by watchmen. It was not uncommon to find boatmen shafting boats in the confines of a wharf to get them away from a loading area to one where the horse or tugs could link up with them. The date of this photograph is the 7 May 1953. It can be seen that the wharf was also rail connected.

122 Though this day boat appears to be only lightly laden, it must have a heavy load situated low down out of sight in the hold, as it is so low in the water. This photograph was taken in the mid 1950s. It would appear that the boat has a single crew member only, as there is nobody walking with the horse. This is the Birmingham main line approaching Deepfields Junction, where, through the bridge, the Wednesbury Oak Loops of Brindley's original Birmingham Canal wound around the hill at Coseley. All that remains now is the section leading to the British Waterways Board's workshop at Bradley, though it used to pass down the nine Bradley Locks to Moorcroft Junction on the Walsall Canal. The locks finally closed in 1961. Ahead of the day boat is a long distance horse boat. The children bathing on the right show that the canal was pretty shallow close to the bank.

123

123 In the heart of the Black Country the coal boats have arrived at their destination; the whole atmosphere of the industrial scene is caught in this photograph. On the left is an unloaded day boat, while a fully loaded boat is being moved by means of a shaft. Another empty boat floats idly across the canal, the very simple decoration (for recognition) of these boats showing on the stern. Behind is the stern end of a long distance boat. Many day boats had the facility of hanging the rudder at either end, so saving them having to be turned round at the end of each trip. There were plenty of winding holes on the Birmingham Canal Navigation, so in practice the rudder was not changed round as often as some people might have thought. The term 'Joey' boat is often applied to the Birmingham area day boats. Usually the 'Joey' boat is one with a cabin.

124 While Joey boats usually kept within the vicinity of the Black Country and Birmingham, they did on occasions do longer runs. One such was down the Staffordshire and Worcestershire Canal to the Electric Light Factory (power

station) at Stourport. Traffic commenced when the station started generating in April 1926. It ceased in June 1949, when a rail connection was laid to the power station and the coal then all came by rail. In this case the run was divided into two parts, with boatmen handing over their boats half way and working back to the coalfields with empty craft. This is Stewponey Wharf in March 1945 with Joey boats loaded with coal on the left, and the Staffordshire, Worcestershire and Shropshire Electric Power Company of Smethwick's boat *James* lying unloaded at the wharfside.

125 In this photograph, thought to have been taken around 1906, a Joey boat has strayed up the Shropshire Union Canal as far as Goldstone Wharf near Market Drayton, some 25 miles from Wolverhampton. This was quite likely an irregular run from the coal fields with fuel to serve a local community and it may have been undertaken by a small carrier rather than a boat from a larger fleet. Whoever owned it, the boat looks in poor condition.

124

Goldstone — The Wharf
Published by Bennion, Horne, Smallman & Co., Ltd., Market Drayton.

125

126

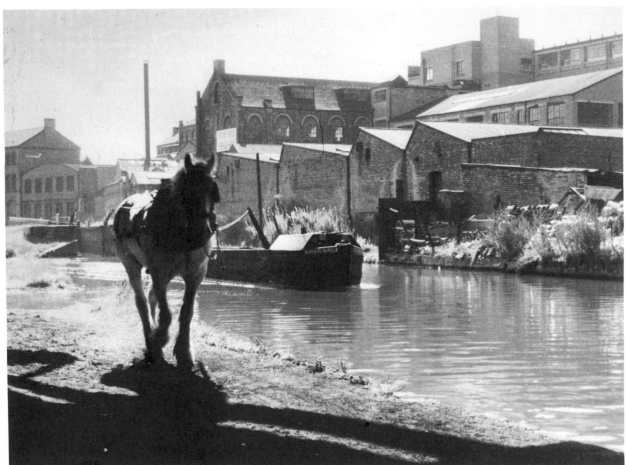

127

126 Much of Birmingham's refuse used to be carried away by canal. It was the first collected by horse and cart and taken to a number of canalside loading points. This is the wharf near Salvage Turn on the Worcester and Birmingham Canal, close to the Gas Street Basin. Rubbish from this wharf was taken to a tip at Lifford. The wharf has a cobbled surface and the elegant gas lamp would now be an object for the collector, whereas at the time the picture was taken, in 1912, it was there for purely functional purposes. This section of the canal was so busy that 24-hour working was necessary and these gas lights were installed for illumination when dark. The builders merchants opposite obviously got their pipes by canal.

127 While some of the refuse was carried by owner-boatmen, most of it was moved by a fleet of boats owned by the Birmingham Corporation's Refuse and Salvage Department, or a contractor such as T. and S. Element. One of the corporation's depots was at Bordesley between locks 54 and 55 on the Camp Hill flight. Much of the refuse from this depot was taken to the BSA tip at Small Heath. In this picture the horse is bringing back an empty boat to the depot and is seen emerging from lock 53. The boat is being towed backwards, but this was no problem due to the fact that the rudder could be hung at either end of the boat. This picture was taken in March 1964 and traffic ceased from the Bordesley depot a year later. Note the leaning towing mast, which would be stepped in different positions to counteract the effect of the wind blowing the boat in or out.

128 The real atmosphere of boating in the Midlands is caught in this photograph of a Thomas Clayton tar boat waiting to descend the twenty-one locks at Wolverhampton. The crew have drawn the paddles and are waiting while the empty lock fills. The tar boat is empty, possibly going to Wolverhampton Gas Works, which was situated part way down the flight, where it could obtain another cargo. The boat has a fore-cabin. The structure on the deck is for the storage of fodder for the horse, spare ropes, etc, and may also have been a kennel for the dog as well. The bricked area surrounding the lock is also typical of an industrial canal on which there was heavy traffic. The raised brickwork would give more grip to the horses' hooves.

129

129 While the Joey, or day boat, was responsible for most of the trade in the built up areas of the Midlands, it must be remembered that long distance boats traded in and out of this industrial area as well. This view is of Cambrian Wharf, Birmingham, at the entrance to the Newhall Branch, better known to most people these days as the top of the Farmer's Bridge flight of locks, which lead out of the picture to the right by the fore end of the nearest boat. The area in the left of the picture has now been almost completely redeveloped, and is best known for the modern Long Boat public house. The Newhall Branch was closed in 1948. The two horse-boats belong to Brierly Hill firms, are called *Elizabeth* and *Four Sisters,* while *Lorna* behind them comes from the Shropshire Union Railways & Canal Company's fleet.

130 These octagonal toll houses situated on small islands were to be found in many places on the Birmingham Canal Navigations. Because the journeys over this network were much shorter, plus the fact that there were many arms and branches, there were a lot of toll collecting points to ensure that each boat paid adequately for the length of its trip and

its cargo. George Arnold with his horse Betty, stops his boat loaded with dry slack at Bromford Stop for gauging and toll paying some time in 1958. George Arnold worked for Ernest Thomas of Walsall. The boat is *Tom No 28* belonging to the Central Electricity Authority. The slack had been loaded at Sandwell Colliery Wharf, Smethwick, bound for Ocker Hill Power Station. This trip was made twice a day for six days a week.

131 When passing through a tunnel with a Birmingham day boat fully laden it was not possible to fit the boat with wings for the leggers. Instead the boatmen lie on the cargo, probably on sacks, and walk the boats through. Also, most tunnels on the Birmingham Canal Navigation (except those with tow paths) were built only eight or nine foot wide. Because of this lack of width, wings were not necessary. This is a photograph of Gosty Hill Tunnel on the Dudley Number 2 Line, coming out into the Stewarts and Lloyds Tube Works, taken early this century. The boat belongs to H.S. Pitt who owned many collieries nearby, and is probably heading for the tube works.

132 One end of the canal at Stewarts and Lloyds plunged straight into the 557-yd Gosty Hill Tunnel, which was too narrow to allow boats to pass and so they were towed through by tug. In later years the coming of motorboats caused the following notice to be put up:

Notice
Private motor tugs and motor boats must enter this end of the tunnel only during the period of ten minutes before or ten minutes after the company tug has entered and the drivers must inform the company's driver of their intention to proceed or follow him.
By order B.C.N.

Gosty Hill Tunnel was busy as a through route until Lappal Tunnel fell in, and afterwards with all the traffic to Stewarts and Lloyds. In this photograph, taken in the early 1930s the tunnel tug *George II* is seen entering at the Dudley end. This tug was unusual in having a propellor at each end, so doing away with the necessity of turning the tug after each journey. The engine was a paraffin fuelled 20hp Bolinder. The building on the left was the overnight 'garage' for the tug. *George II* was sols in 1935 and not replaced. Ventilation was always a problem in this tunnel.

134

133 Having just emerged from Gosty Hill Tunnel, this Stewarts and Lloyds tug is stemming four Joey boats back to the collieries for more coal. Stemming is the close-linked towing of boats where stem overlaps stern. In this way, fewer steerers are required, though the second boat needed a steerer using reverse helm. The photograph was taken near Station Road Bridge, Old Hill, one chilly February day in 1956. Stewarts and Lloyds owned four tugs in all. The Joey boat moored on the left is also owned by the steel works, and has their name on the counter. Some of the Stewarts and Lloyds boats were specially constructed without any cross bracing in the hold so that they could carry the full length of manufactured tubes. While we usually refer to the open boats of the Birmingham Canal Navigation system as Joey boats, many boatmen in the area just referred to them as barges!

134 There were long stretches of lock-free canal in and around Birmingham and so it was sensible to employ tugs on certain of these routes if there was regular traffic. Chance & Hunt Limited of Oldbury had a fleet of boats carrying chemicals and in 1919 ordered two powerful tugs, the *Stentor* and the *Hector* from the famous boat builders Walkers of Rickmansworth. These were the first motor tugs on the Birmingham Canal Navigation. This photograph was taken outside their yard just prior to delivery. These tugs were fitted with 25hp Bolinder engines and were more elaborately fitted out than most tugs, having sleeping accommodation in a cabin at the fore-end. It would appear that the layout of the cabin is the same as one would expect at the rear of a boat, only in this case the cabin doors opened forwards. The steamer type funnel is unusual on a narrowboat.

135 In order to feed the railways, some railway companies built a special type of day boat for taking products from factories to the canal/rail interchange sidings. The Midland Railway, the LNWR, and the GWR each operated a fleet of these boats around Birmingham where they were called 'railway' or 'station' boats. On nationalisation of the railways in 1948, these few boats were retained under British Railways ownership and did not pass into the hands of British Waterways. Many of these boats had very fine lines, more akin to a long distance boat, but usually without a cabin. The helm and tiller had the looks of a long distance boat as well. After the cessation of this railway traffic a number had cabins built on them, and were converted for long haul work. This photograph shows the last cargo of bricks being taken to Bloomfield interchange at Tipton, in 1952. This was one of the craft built for the LMS (successors to the Midland Railway) by W. J. Yarwood and Sons Ltd of Northwich. No 22 denotes *Rhine*, a steel boat delivered in January 1938.

135

136 The longest type of narrow craft regularly trading on the canals were the Wolverhampton boats (known as 'ampton or wharf boats) which measured 87ft long by 7ft 9in beam. They could carry up to 50 tons of cargo. These boats traded on the lock-free waters between the collieries at Cannock and Anglesey Basin, the Wolverhampton area and southwards to Tipton. They were often towed in trains of three, four, or even five, behind a motorised tug. In this photograph of a Sunday School outing taken in the late 1930s a Wolverhampton boat belonging to C.W. Mitchard Coal Merchants and Canal Steerers, is seen leaving Owen Street Wharf, Tipton. The party are being towed by that firm's tug *Jubilee,* formerly the double ended tunnel tug *George II* from Gosty Hill Tunnel.

137 One of the last traffics on the canals of Birmingham was a short haul run from the chemical works of Allbright and Wilson down Brades Hall Locks to a discharging point at Dudley Port. Alfred Matty & Sons, long established tug and boat owners, were responsible for this, transporting phosphorus in solution. Because of the corrosive nature of some of the cargo, wooden boats were preferred. Alfred Matty appears to pay no tribute to tradition; the cabins are painted a light yellow, and there is no trace of the familiar roses and castles, neither is the water can decorated in any way.

138 In 1950 the last commercial boat passed through
Dudley Tunnel and in 1962 it was officially abandoned.
Thanks to the efforts of the Dudley Tunnel Preservation
Society (now the Dudley Canal Trust) the tunnel has been
repaired and was re-opened in 1973. It is now the longest
canal tunnel in Britain still useable, being 3,154yd long,
and part of it is un-lined and hewn through solid rock.
The tunnel carried a great deal of trade in its day; in 1853
for example, 41,704 boats passed through the tunnel. In
order to stimulate interest in the preservation project, the
Dudley Tunnel Preservation Society ran trips through the
tunnel in one of the wooden Joey boats. This trip was in
1964, and shows the Tipton portal of the tunnel. The
railway over the top was formerly the GWR and the
locomotive crossing it is one of the Hall Class. This stretch
of track is now purely a head-shunt for the nearby
Freightliner depot. The name of the previous owner of
the boat (M.S. Tonks) still appears on its side.

139 As trade declined in the Midlands, most of the day
boats were scrapped or abandoned. It is now very difficult
to find examples of certain of these craft for preservation
by museums and societies. In this case there was a slightly
happier ending. These five boats are on their way from
Birmingham, via the Grand Union Canal, to be converted
into house boats and moored on the lower reaches of the
Basingstoke Canal. This picture was taken in July 1959
near Wood Lock. The British Waterways narrowboat
towing the five boats only employed a crew of three. They
must have had to work hard down Hatton Flight and up
the other side, to say nothing of the locks up and down
from the Tring Summit.

7 BOATS AND BOAT BUILDING

140

140 Boat building and repair was an important canalside activity. There were very many private yards up and down the country, as well as the ones owned by the big fleet operators. This is one of the latter; the Anderton Company's premises at Middleport, Burslem, on the Trent and Mersey Canal. In this dock boats would be both built and repaired. As was common narrow canal practice, the boats were built or repaired parallel with the water. The boats were usually pulled up out of the water along greased rails or planks. At the Anderton Yard there was an electric hoist which actually lifted the boats bodily — this was probably one of the most efficient docks on the canal system. The Anderton Company boats always had their names carved into the top plank at the stern as with *Cymric*.

141 Another large dock was that run by Fellows Morton & Clayton at Saltley, Birmingham, approximately half way down the locks known as Garrison Flight. In this photograph taken in 1897 four horse-drawn boats are under repair under cover of the roof of the building shed. Two other boats lie alongside. A horse-drawn narrowboat would take about six weeks to build and need eight people working on it full time. In the 1920s it would have cost around £225. In this picture a new steam powered narrowboat is being built in the foreground. It is of composite construction with an elm bottom and would shortly be fitted with wrought iron sides. The cost of the eleven steamers built in this yard between 1896 and 1899 averaged out at £560 each.

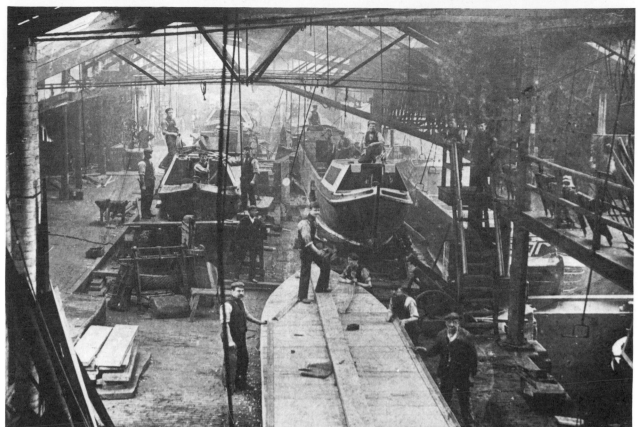

141

142

142 Boats were not always built by recognised boatyards. The Regents Canal Company for example had a pair of boats built in 1929 by a firm with the unlikely name of the Steel Barrel Company of Uxbridge. These were the famous pair called *George* and *Mary*. The slightly unusual narrowboat in this picture was built by the London and North-Western Railway at their Crewe works. It is assumed that it was for use on the Shropshire Union Canal, which was under that railway's control; the style of lettering on the stern also suggests the Shropshire Union Canal. The boat is of all metal construction including the cabin, which meant that unless it was well insulated it would suffer from condensation. It is thought that this boat could have been built for maintenance purposes. The fore cabin was for tools while the cabin at the rear was just a mess room. It had a very unusual arrangement for hanging the rudder.

143

143 Possibly the largest yard in Britain latterly employed on building working narrowboats was that of W.J. Yarwood & Sons Ltd of Northwich, on the River Weaver. In 1896 they took over an existing yard and for the next 30 years concentrated mainly on building river craft. However, during the late 1920s and '30s they also built steel narrowboats, many for Fellows Morton & Clayton and the Grand Union Canal Carrying Company. A total of sixty-two narrowboats were built for the latter company alone — welcome orders in the slack 1930s. This picture was taken in late February 1935, and besides the river craft on the slips there are four narrowboats. These were the first of a batch of ten motorboats built for Fellows Morton and Clayton. In order of commissioning they were *Cactus, Clematis, Clover, Cypress, Roach, Rudd, Shad, Skate, Tench* and *Trout.*

144 Thomas Clayton of Oldbury had their depot and boatyard at Tat Bank Road, Oldbury. This photograph was taken in 1964 two years before the company ceased its activities. Here the motorboat *Tay* is on the slip undergoing repair. In this boatyard there is no fully covered slip, the corrugated iron sheds at either end of the

boat are moveable so that in inclement weather the majority of the boat can be covered, or just the section under repair. As can be seen from some of the boats in the foreground, Thomas Clayton were letting a number of their fleet fall into disrepair, presumably as trade declined. The firm usually had their name in full on the cabin side, but towards the end changed it to TC(O) Limited on some craft.

145 The atmosphere of the country boatyard is well captured in this picture, which is believed to have been taken in 1890. It shows the old Erewash Canal Dock at Narrow, or Packhorse, Bridge, near Trent Lock. In the early days of the canal the Company owned four docks of which this was one, but by 1792 they had leased it out. At the time that this picture was taken, it was owned by the Tinsdale family. The actual dock is on the right between the two huts, at right-angles to the canal. The waterway has been widened at this point to allow boats to be launched across the width of the canal. The timber stacked around the huts is there seasoning. The wide boat in the background is an upper Trent boat, possibly once sailed, using a simple square sail, like a keel.

144

145

146

146 Another famous boat builder was Nurser of Braunston, who started business around 1870. William Nurser had a country-wide reputation and built boats for northern carriers such as Henry Seddon of Middlewich, and John Green, a carrier from Macclesfield. Nearer to home they built for Samuel Barlow Coal Co, Fellows Morton & Clayton, and Thomas Clayton (Oldbury) Ltd. As trade declined so there was less building of new boats and more repairs. After selling out to the Samuel Barlow Coal Company in 1941 the yard was used mainly for repairs, though new boats were occasionally built there, including the last wooden trading boat *Raymond* in 1958. This is a war-time photograph of work taking place on the Samuel Barlow motorboat *Hardy*. The boat is in a dry dock. *Hardy* was built by Nurser at Braunston in 1940. A number of yards built and repaired in dry dock rather than have any form of a slip.

147 The end of an era — the last wooden working narrowboat is launched at Braunston for the Samuel Barlow Coal Company. The butty *Raymond* was launched sideways in the traditional manner in the summer of 1958. *Raymond* went on to become one of the last narrowboats trading, as part of the Blue Line Fleet, skippered by

Arthur Bray with his wife Rose and son Ernest Kendall. It looks as if the boat was built without provision for a cabin stove or chimney, but all subsequent photographs show that they were fitted. All the decorative painting was by the yard's own painter, Ron Hough.

148 The last wooden motorboat to be built at Barlow's dock at Braunston was the short boat *Trees* built in 1961. This boat was built for use as a leisure boat and was later finished with a cabin over its full length. The lack of any modern tools is very apparent, though the electric cable leads one to suppose that they might be using an electric drill. Boat building would have changed very little over the 200 years since the first canal was built. In this case metal knees are being used whereas wooden ones would have been used originally. Note the stern counter made from one block of wood, and the planks being held in their newly bent position by clamps. Wooden boats usually had oak sides, which on a trading boat would have been alternatively wet and dry, depending whether the boat was loaded or not. The bottoms were of elm which lasts for a long time in a water-logged state, and usually they wore thin before failing for other reasons.

147

148

149 A boat building firm popular with the number-ones of the Midlands was that of Lees and Atkins of Polesworth, on the Coventry Canal. An owner boatman would set aside a little money from each trip calling it his docking money. This is the money he would use for repairs and repainting when they were required for his boat. Under normal circumstances a wooden boat would require docking every three years and would possibly have a life of 30 years. Unless the boatman took his holiday during the one or two weeks that his boat was in dock, he stood to lose income, so the boatyard would often hire him a 'change boat' which belonged to them. In the 1920s the hire charge was approximately 11s per week. This photograph dated 1910 was taken by Temple-Thurston on his travels, and shows a Lees and Atkins change boat in use.

150 As we have seen previously, most tunnels were built without towpaths. With the coming of steam it was thought that this power could be harnessed to pull boats through a tunnel on an endless rope principle. As an experiment, the Grand Junction Company installed a wire rope haulage system in Braunston Tunnel in October 1870. Within a month it had proved unworkable, possibly due to excessive friction inside the 2,042yd-long tunnel. By the following February a steam tug had been ordered which arrived in April, and there was another for the nearby Blisworth Tunnel. The professional leggers were then paid off and each received a pension of 5s per week. This photograph, taken at 4.30 in the afternoon of an August day in 1907, shows the tunnel tug with a full head of steam having just turned round after its last trip, approaching a line of waiting boats at the Welton end of the Braunston Tunnel.

151 The tunnel tugs worked to a timetable. The Braunston tug provided an hourly service through the tunnel, while at nearby Blisworth (a longer tunnel) it was every hour and a half. The charge when the tugs were first introduced was 1s 6d for laden boats, 1s 3d for partially laden boats, and 1s for empties. A tug could pull up to twenty narrowboats at a time. While steam tugs remained until the end on these two major tunnels, on the Grand Union Canal motor tugs were being used from 1908 on the Worcester and Birmingham Canal tunnels. This photograph taken in 1914 shows horsedrawn boats awaiting the arrival of the tunnel tugs at the Welton end of the Braunston Tunnel. The narrowboat in the foreground is unusual, having a very short foredeck.

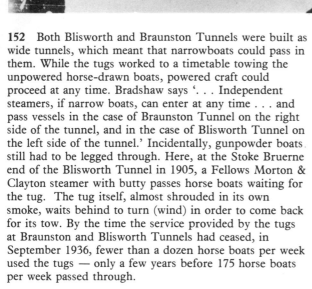

152 Both Blisworth and Braunston Tunnels were built as wide tunnels, which meant that narrowboats could pass in them. While the tugs worked to a timetable towing the unpowered horse-drawn boats, powered craft could proceed at any time. Bradshaw says '. . . Independent steamers, if narrow boats, can enter at any time . . . and pass vessels in the case of Braunston Tunnel on the right side of the tunnel, and in the case of Blisworth Tunnel on the left side of the tunnel.' Incidentally, gunpowder boats still had to be legged through. Here, at the Stoke Bruerne end of the Blisworth Tunnel in 1905, a Fellows Morton & Clayton steamer with butty passes horse boats waiting for the tug. The tug itself, almost shrouded in its own smoke, waits behind to turn (wind) in order to come back for its tow. By the time the service provided by the tugs at Braunston and Blisworth Tunnels had ceased, in September 1936, fewer than a dozen horse boats per week used the tugs — only a few years before 175 horse boats per week passed through.

153 Tugs came to the tunnels at Preston Brook, Barnton and Saltersford on the Trent and Mersey in 1864. While Preston Brook Tunnel (1,239yd) was straight, a surveying fault in the other two had left them with a pronounced bend which caused some problems with steering in the darkness because of the poor head lamps on the boats. The two tugs which regularly worked these tunnels were fitted with spring-loaded guide wheels, two at the fore-end and two at the stern. These wheels could be locked into position to give the necessary guidance, so doing away with the necessity for a steersman when the boat was in the tunnels. Because these two tunnels were close together they were worked as one. In this undated photograph the tunnel tug is emerging from Barnton Tunnel and the guide wheels are clearly seen. These tugs were finally withdrawn from service in 1943.

154 Horse boat *Willie* is just about to enter Preston Brook Tunnel in tow behind the tunnel tug. This is a Runcorn type narrowboat built six planks deep instead of the usual five, which would allow it to carry extra cargoes on the deeper waterways around Manchester. Because of the extra height of the sides, the cabin has been built that much lower. Both boats are fitted with timberheads as well as studs which was common practice on Runcorn boats which were often towed in pairs by Bridgewater tugs.

153

154

155

155 An electric tug was used at the Harecastle Tunnel on the Trent and Mersey Canal. Once the original Brindley Tunnel became impassable it was essential that traffic should pass as quickly as possible through the other bore. Because of ventilation problems, an electric tug was used which hauled itself along on a cable on the tunnel floor. For many years the boat was powered by batteries contained in a second boat close behind. Later this boat was done away with, and current was collected from an overhead trolley line. This is the Chatterly end of the tunnel before the overhead wires were put up, the tug and its battery boat are on the left. The first boat to have been towed through on this trip belonged to the Trent and Mersey number-one Jim Hollingshead who is seen standing with his horse.

156 Charringtons the coal merchants once ran a fleet of five steam tugs in and around London. Most of them were employed moving lighters loaded with coal up from Limehouse Dock to Kensal and other gas works. As with the tug already illustrated which worked on the Birmingham Canal Navigation, there is a living cabin at the fore end, complete with cabin stove. While all the waterways which would have been worked by this tug were wide, Charringtons (and other firms) favoured narrow beam tugs because they could often be bought second-hand from the canal companies. Also, they could wind anywhere on a wide waterway, which made them very flexible in operation.

157 It was usually commonplace for the directors of a canal company to inspect their waterway at least once a year. The company would normally keep a special boat just for this purpose, and other VIP uses. One of the most splendid was *Inspector* based at Ellesmere maintenance yard, for use on the Ellesmere section of the Shropshire Union Canal. This photograph shows the inspection party waiting to board *Inspector* on the 22 June 1900, at Colemere near Ellesmere. It is interesting to see the 'S' shaped structure at the bow; a symbolic reminder of the days when express or fly boats had a sharp knife mounted at the bow to cut the tow lines of any slower craft that did not give way to them. While it looks as if *Inspector* might be motorised, the rear part of the cabin with louvred doors was the galley — not an engine room; it was a horsedrawn boat. The second craft is an ordinary trading or maintenance boat (fitted with a bow cabin) especially done up for the occasion. *Inspector* was used until 1934 after which it passed into private hands.

158 It was not usual for senior canal personnel to have boats allocated to them. An exception however was T.W. Milner, Engineer of the northern district of the Grand Junction Canal. He held this post from 1896 through to 1930, and during this time he used a Bradbury motorcycle for business transport as well as a second-hand Belsize car. On the water, however, he used this splendid looking clinker-built steam launch *Gadfly*, on this occasion being used for a social outing. It is unlikely that Mr Milner features in the photograph, as he was an official photographer for the canal company. Happily, most of his photographs are preserved at the Waterways Museum at Stoke Bruerne.

159 From the very early days the Duke of Bridgewater arranged for packet boats to run on his canal. These were fast craft built to finer lines than others for the conveyance of passengers and light or perishable cargo. They usually ran 'fly', meaning that they ran non-stop and other boats had to get out of their way, or risk having their tow-lines cut. A similar boat was the *Duchess Countess* a narrowboat with very fine lines which was still running as late as 1924, not by this time as a fly boat, but running between Knott Mill and Stockton carrying light cargoes and parcels. This photograph was taken at Lymm in 1904 and shows the crew of three from the *Duchess Countess*.

160

160 After coming out of service in 1924 the *Duchess Countess* sank. Later she was raised and travelled to Frankton Junction on the Llangollen Canal where she was used as a house boat. Later, as she became more decrepit she was put up on the bank. These photographs were taken in the late 1940s before the boat was finally broken up. The very fine lines of the bow on this fast boat can be clearly seen. The cabin in the centre was an addition by the recluse who lived in her for her latter years.

161 At one time, one of the most important boats in the canal company's fleet was the ice breaker. These boats were originally made of wood, sheathed in metal, and were used in times of freezing weather to clear a path through the frozen canal to free trapped trading boats. A gang of men would stand either end of the bar amidships as seen here; a number of horses would pull the ice breaker through the ice, while at the same time these men would rock it from side to side. The steersman would also steer an erratic course, so breaking up the maximum amount of ice. This is the Shropshire Union Canal Co's icebreaker *Audlem*, at Audlem Wharf around 1900. On this canal the main company-owned wharves had their own ice breaking boat, always named after its home mooring. The building behind was 'the company's' warehouse with, to the right, accommodation for the warehouseman, and above a small chapel for the boat people. There is a local legend that a young person was murdered on the steps of the chapel years ago, and the blood stains on the steps would return whenever they were washed! The building is now well known to holiday makers as the Shroppie Fly public house. Next door there used to be a mill which has now been expertly converted into a shop and craft centre by that well known enthusiast John Stothert.

162 One of the worst winters ever known on the canal system was that of 1894-5. During this period of cold weather it was impossible to keep many of the canals open with the horsedrawn ice breakers. From this photograph it can be seen that many men and horses are required for a successful ice breaking operation. This scene is on the Birmingham main line at Dudley Port Junction. In this case, the ice having been broken by the boat, it was collected and piled on the bank to stop it re-freezing in the waterway. During this freeze a bizarre experiment took place when a boat containing a huge boiler and pump equipment was used to pump boiling water back into the canal. Experts calculated it was capable of thawing ice at least a mile each side of the boat. The machine brought forth many jokes — all justified. It failed dismally — one night the fire went out and the water in the boiler froze —it stayed that way for ten weeks!

163 These boats were iced up on the Grand Union Canal at Acocks Green, near Cartwright's Timber Yard, in 1929. The ice around the boats is snow covered and the boats are quite immovable. These boatmen are lucky, they have become iced up within a few yards of civilisation, but often boats would become iced in on remote stretches of canal, and the crews would have to walk through thick snow to find any form of provisions. The old style ice breaker gradually became less used for a number of reasons. The main reason was that they became superseded by all-metal hulls which could break a much thicker layer of ice. A horse-drawn boat could not break more than four inches. A motorised metal hulled boat had more chance of pushing through the ice than a horse-drawn boat, and could of course easily back off and have another run at it. The more modern powerful tugs used by maintenance staff were far more effective ice breaking tools than the horse-drawn ice breaker, and required far less crew and no horses! Also one suspects that the winters are not quite so severe this century.

164 A real frosty morning on the Trent and Mersey Canal at Stenson, near Derby, in 1940, with Fellows Morton & Clayton motorboat *Monarch* and butty *Romford* iced up. Moving forward was not the only problem created by ice; working through locks became a slow process, as lumps of ice would become jammed behind the lock gates, so hindering a boat entering the lock; and ice could jam between the sides of the boat and the lockside, leaving a boat immovable. Ice could also block the paddle openings. An additional problem in horse-drawn days was the state of the tow path which could be so covered in ice that it was a danger to the horse, as well as giving little grip. Even sacking tied around the horses hooves gave only a little extra grip. Sometimes horses were shod with specially pointed frost nails.

165 Dredging is a very important part of canal maintenance and takes up a great deal of time and money. In earlier times dredging was crude and relatively inefficient. It often consisted of the spoon dredger, similar to the one illustrated here, working on the Trent and Mersey Canal in 1900. Here a spoon dredging system has been mounted more or less permanently on a maintenance narrowboat. The spoon is mounted on the end of a long shaft, which is controlled by the man standing by the cabin. When the spoon, or scoop, is full it is raised by the crane mechanism mounted amidships. In this case the dredgings are carried forward into the hold of the dredger which then moves off to the unloading point. Spoon dredgers were still in use in the 1940s, when one boatman remarked 'All they do is muck about with a bloody big spoon. Dredging! These days they ought to have a machine. Spoonin' it out is useless. . . .' (From *Hold on a Minute* by T. Wilkinson).

166 With the coming of steam, a number of different dredging systems were introduced. In this case the Thames Conservancy have taken two narrowboats and mounted on them a steam grab crane. Presumably this was operating on a stretch of the River Thames where low bridges were not a problem. Vertical boilered dredgers were not common on canals because of the low headroom. In this case the dredgings have been placed on the bank — they usually had to be taken away by other boats.

168 One of the problems with a dredger on a narrow canal was that it needed to be mounted on a wide hull, so as to gain stability, otherwise it would topple over. One of the commonest ways of getting over this problem was to mount the dredger on a narrow hull and when dredging started the dredging gang would fix a pontoon on each side of the hull so doubling its width.This ex-Shropshire Union Railway and Canal Company dredger has been so assembled and was photographed near Nantwich in 1954. This is a Grafton dredger with a boom for accurate placing of the grab; this type was first supplied to the Grand Junction in 1894 and subsequently became very popular with canal companies. The accompanying mud boat is a very decrepit ex-working boat. The tall chimney of the dredger could be lowered as could the jib of the crane for passing under bridges.

167 This photograph taken in 1918 shows a dredging team at work, again on the Thames, this time at Nags Head Island, Abingdon. This Grafton grab dredger is no makeshift affair but a purpose built wide dredger. They are, however, using narrowboats as mud boats. The boat in the foreground is a purpose built hopper, having no cabin and high sides, while the one on the left beside the dredger is a conventional horse-drawn narrowboat complete with cabin. On the right of the picture is a steam tug, presumably for towing the mud boats away to the point at which they will be unloaded. It is interesting to see that the dredger is showing a warning flag for the benefit of other river users, indicating which side they may pass.

169 It is very unlikely that the London and North Eastern Railway really wanted the Macclesfield Canal, but they inherited it together with others, such as the Peak Forest and the Ashton, from the Great Central Railway. Having acquired them, they had to maintain them. This is the horse-drawn maintenance boat *Henry* fitted with an extended cabin for messing purposes. This picture was taken four months before the railways were nationalised in 1948 at Buxton Road Wharf, Macclesfield.

170 In the early autumn of 1942 a culvert collapsed in one of the great Telford embankments on the Shropshire Union Canal at Shebdon. This required a major repair which closed the canal to through traffic for a number of months. While this repair was going on, the opportunity was taken to drain the canal in a number of other places for maintenance to take place. Here, just south of Nantwich Basin, repairs are being carried out on the embankment which skirts the town. A maintenance boat has been deliberately grounded in the canal, and is being used to support wheel-barrow runs, also to act as a mess room. The 'V' formation of the canal bed and channel already described in this book are clearly shown, as is the reason for the instruction to 'hold out' on a bend, as there is more depth of water on the outside.

171 There are many different craft required for the maintenance of the waterways. This photograph shows a steam pump. It is a specially made craft and unusually the cabin, which is only a mess room, is at the fore-end. The engine driving the pump is similar to stationary or portable steam engines commonly found at that time in use on farms or in industry. The pump is being used to drain water from the inside of a coffer dam, which is protecting some new construction works. The scene is the lower Grand Union Canal in 1907 when a 200ft length of waterway wall was being installed for the Hayes Development Company. The pump boat comes from Bulbourne which has always been a Grand Union maintenance yard. In the distance, coming towards the camera, is a steam boat with butty.

8 CANALS IN WARTIME

During World War I a number of canals were allowed to go into decline. At the commencement of the war, all the railway owned canals were immediately put under the control of the Railway Executive Committee, and kept their labour force more or less intact. The other canals which were independent received little help, and many of their able-bodied staff or boatmen were called up to serve in the forces, or left to work in the munitions industry where the wages were higher. Eventually it was realised that all canals could help with the war effort, and in particular they could take some pressure off the over-worked railways. In March 1917 the Board of Trade formed a Canal Control Committee to get traffic moving again on the waterways system, in many cases using troops as boatmen.

While the Kennet and Avon Canal did not see a great deal of traffic during World War I, even though it had come under State control as it was railway owned, some army manoeuvres and training did take place on it near Devizes, but this was mainly training troops in the use of barges, so that they could take over such duties required on the waterways of the Continent.

The Board of Trade through the Canal Control Committee took over two narrowboats on the Kennet and Avon, named the *Essex* and *Bedford*, and used these

for training purposes for eventual use on other canals. These photographs, believed to have been taken for publicity purposes, show some of the training. The men are from the Royal Engineers (Inland Waterways Transport Section) who were the group trained to operate barges as described previously. The boats are obviously a pair used for working out on to the Thames, because of the substantial wash-boards at the bows. One other aspect of the war was that all able-bodied horses were called up for use at the front, which left many canal carriers badly depleted. The notes received with these photographs from the Imperial War Museum state that all the horses used in the exercise here were unfit for general military service.

172 Lower wharf Devizes, just above the top lock.

173 Top lock at Devizes. The pleasure boats were operated by a Mr King who ceased business during the 1930s.

174 Between locks 48 and 49 at Devizes. The Devizes swimming pool (which used canal water) is seen behind. Note the Board of Trade (B↑T) and Canal Control Committee (CCC) abbreviations on the boat.

173

174

175 By the time of World War I, the Basingstoke Canal was very run down, and the top end to Basingstoke was derelict. During the war the canal came under the control of the War Office and was run by the Royal Engineers. Most of the cargoes were for the camps at Aldershot, many coming from the stores at Woolwich. Return traffic was mainly timber from Frimley and Fleet. In this picture taken in 1916, German prisoners of war are seen loading timber on to A.J. Harmsworth's boat *Dauntless* built new for Harmsworth in 1905 at Berkhamstead. Horse manure was also a return cargo! From 1923 to 1948 the Harmsworth family owned the canal and were the principal carriers on it.

176 During this war the Red Cross became boat owners and carriers on the Kennet and Avon Canal. They purchased a narrowboat called *Bittern* to use as a hospital craft. This was used as a day trip boat between a hospital at Winsley and Bradford-on-Avon. The boat was painted in Red Cross colours and rigged out with a simple awning over the main part of the hold. Often the boat was run by one boatman, with lady helpers, possibly from the hospital. In 1920 the independent canals were returned to their owners, but both the railway owned waterways and the independents had suffered a great deal due to lack of maintenance; in some cases they never recovered from it.

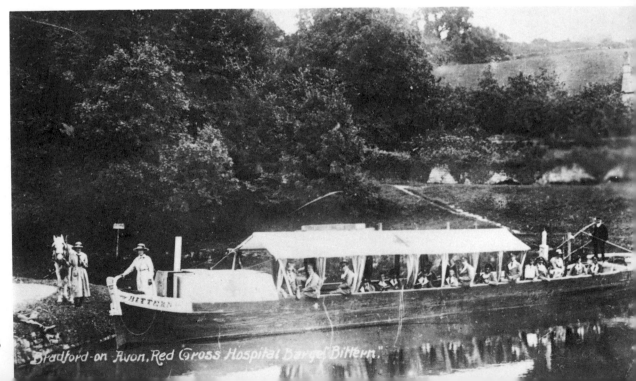

177 With the coming of World War II the railway owned canals became the responsibility of the Ministry of Transport. The independent waterways remained on their own until 1942. Some of the younger boatmen were called up but later canal boatmen became a 'reserved occupation' as it was realised that the waterways could provide a useful alternative to other forms of transport. In this early 1940s photograph from the archives of the Imperial War Museum a pair of Grand Union Canal Carrying Co boats are seen on the flight of locks leading up to Stoke Bruerne (Lock 18). They had probably taken a load of coal from the Warwickshire coal fields to a coal yard in London, and, unable to obtain a return load, were having to go back empty. Many canal carriers lost their usual cargoes due to their non availability in war conditions. Another problem concerned the change in pattern of deep sea ships who were often diverted from normal ports of call to ones which were not served by canals.

178 To fill the gaps created by the calling up of the younger boatmen, the Grand Union Canal Carrying Company found it necessary to recruit girl volunteers. This experiment was partially successful. The girls were trained by Miss Kitty Gayford, seen on the left, along with (from left to right) Audrey, Evelyn, Mary, Frankie and Anne. This picture was taken at a press photo call on 31 March 1944. Miss Gayford said 'I know it was a special occasion for the press, we were not usually so smart.' The girls are seen on butty *Dipper* and motorboat *Sun*.

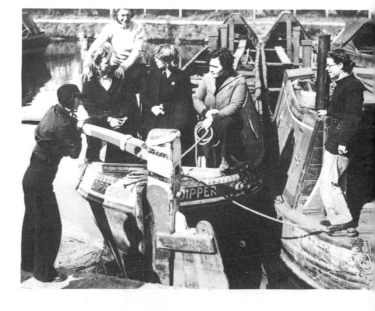

179 On 1 January 1944 over 11,000 people were working on the canals compared with 12,794 before the war; there were however not enough boat builders and boat repairers and of course not enough boatmen (boat persons?), hence the training scheme for the girls who came from all walks of life; most were very individualistic. One such was Pick, seen here at the helm of a motorboat by the turnover bridge No 134 in the middle of Tring Cutting. She regularly smoked a pipe — puffing away at it as naturally as if it was a cigarette. Beside the bicycle is a drab water can; the chimney too is undecorated having no brass rings around it. The butty is keeping to one side in order to see ahead, as well as keeping out of the wash of the motor.

180 The caption on this press photograph reads:

Bringing Coal to London, Women Canal 'Boatees' open Winter Campaign

Many Londoners who will not freeze this winter will owe it to the hard work of a gallant band of women volunteers who bring coal to London in canal barges, or, as they prefer to call them, narrowboats. They have received special training for this tough job and now they are navigating the canals in all weathers. They have to operate the locks themselves, to manoeuvre heavily loaded boats in shallow waters, to navigate tricky bends, etc. They eat and sleep aboard, in their tiny cabins.

The skipper of this pair was Mrs Helen Skyrme, wife of a naval officer; she now lives in Wiltshire. Her mate was Olga Kavelos, daughter of a Greek Birmingham restauranteur. This is bridge 184 immediately down stream of Uxbridge Lock.

181 Kitty Gayford teaching a trainee how to splice a rope. In this photograph they are not wearing their badges. Kitty Gayford still has a collection of Grand Union Canal Company cloth insignia as well as the blue and white enamel badge with the motto of the company in the centre, and 'on national service' around the edge. Kitty Gayford was awarded an MBE for her work on canals in wartime. In all some thirty girls were trained and ten pairs of boats were run by them. Despite the efforts of the public relations division of the Ministry, few suitable recruits came forward.

182 During the months succeeding D Day, traffic on the canals declined partly because of diversions of traffic resulting from the military operations, and also because of an acute water shortage on some canals. By autumn 1944 there was spare capacity on the Aire and Calder Navigation and the Grand Union. Here in late 1944 we see a pair of boats locking down in the top lock at Stoke Bruerne. An unidentified trainee poses for the photographer — her picture eventually finding its way into the archives of the Imperial War Museum. Trousers were not worn by the regular boatwomen at this time, but most of the trainees wore trousers, slacks or overalls.

183

183 A lot has been written about the trainees during the last war; their numbers and their importance has possibly been exaggerated — they made an interesting but relatively minor contribution. A similar scheme was tried for men in 1948, in lieu of National Service, but it met with no success at all. Evelyn, Anne and Audrey pose at Bulls Bridge layby near Southall on the Grand Union Canal on 31 March 1944 for a press photograph. The butty *Dipper* was delivered new in December 1935.

184

184 During the war boatmen were given emergency ration cards, along with their ordinary cards, but often had difficulty with buying food as they were never 'regular customers' at any one shop. On a few occasions when the boats went out on to tidal waters they were entitled to seamen's rations as well. This photograph is believed to have been taken in the Control Office at Bulls Bridge, but quite why the wartime rations are on show is not known. Boatmen cannot remember being issued with them from this office. Miss Gayford well remembers buying 'boaters' pies' in the Fishery Inn at Boxmoor!

185 Normally the famous fleet of boats owned by the Ovaltine Factory only carried coal from the Warwickshire coal fields to the factory at Kings Langley, returning empty. In order to gain better carrying capacity during the war, the Grand Union Canal Carrying Co often managed to find back loadings for the independent carriers. In this photograph the Ovaltine boats lie fully loaded, well off their usual route, at Sampson Road Wharf, Birmingham. In the foreground other boats unload barrels, possibly of beer. For protection of perishable cargoes some wharves had covered awnings built out over the canal. The electric overhead hoist and gantry was installed by the Grand Union Canal Co in the modernisation of the 1930s.

186 While quite a number of bombs fell on the British canal system during World War II, relatively few narrowboats were actually hit; photographs of them are very rare. This well known photograph was taken on the 1 November 1940 when a bomb had dropped on New Warwick Wharf in Birmingham. Two pairs of boats were sunk by this direct hit. Motorboat *Robin* and butty *Kildare* were carrying steel tubes to London from Coombeswood. The other pair were motor *Rover* and butty *Grace* fully loaded with cocoa destined for Manchester.

187

187 On 1 January 1948 the canals of Britain were nationalised. The Docks and Inland Waterways Executive was formed to administer the canals, docks and navigable rivers; they also took over all the carrying companies which had previously been owned by individual canal companies. From the start they were known as 'British Waterways' for short. Initially their house colours were bright yellow with blue lettering, a colour-scheme dreamed up by Robert Davidson, a member of the Executive; it had no affinity with any of the traditional colours of the canals. In this picture at least one of the crews have tried to keep up the tradition with roses decorations on the water cans. Here we see motorboat *Darley* and butty *Ayr* after coming up the Thames on a test run; both boats are from the former Grand Union Canal Carrying Co a fleet which formed the basis of British Waterways carrying on canals of the Midlands and the south. Rather than keep taking down the extended tall pipe on the motorboat because of low bridges, it has been taken off and is stowed in front of the cabin. A short exhaust deflector has been substituted. The two chimneys from the cabin stove could be lifted off from the base and are in reach of the crew, and so can be raised and lowered as required. On the wharf in the background are barrels of lime juice waiting carriage up to Boxmoor, a traffic which at the time of writing is still carried by narrowboat.

188 British Transport Waterways took over from the Docks and Inland Waterways Executive on 1 January 1955 and then the colour-scheme changed to one predominantly blue with yellow lettering. Their symbol of a life-buoy and waves was usually featured on the cabin sides as well. On the 1 January 1963 it all changed again to become the British Waterways Board. The roses and castles on the rear doors of the cabin were transfers, and in this case the boatman has a water can painted in British Waterways colours. *Yeoford* was again one of the motorboats formerly in the fleet of the Grand Union Canal Carrying Company. This photograph was taken on the River Nene at Weston Lock and the boats are on their way to Whitworth's Flour Mill at Wellingborough, with a cargo of grain. Grain from Tilbury to Wellingborough was a water-borne cargo for many years. In 1948 a boatman could earn £18 4s 0d per week without having to work too hard. £30 could be obtained with longer hours.

189 One of the first decisions made by the British Waterways Board when they were formed in 1963 was to give up virtually all carrying. By that time many contracts had been lost or transferred to road transport. They kept a few boats to honour two contracts: the lime juice run from Brentford to Boxmoor, and the cement run. This picture taken in the late 1960s shows two boats retained for the latter run from Long Itchington to Sampson Road depot in Birmingham. By this time the boats were looking very tatty and were in poor condition. Sampson Road Wharf too was looking very uncared for — compare this picture with one taken when the Grand Union Canal Co were having a revival of trade in the 1930s. The boats are *Banstead* and *Tow*.

190 Samuel Barlow Coal Company Limited specialised in the transportation of coal. After World War II, they faced stern competition from road transport. They were not nationalised in 1948. In the 1950s in an effort to gain more coal contracts, they took over a number of small carrying firms, some of whom were ailing, but who still had some contracts. One such firm to be taken over was A. Harvey-Taylor of Aylesbury. In this photograph, the Samuel Barlow motorboat *Cairo* is paired with the ex- Harvey-Taylor butty *Daphne* before the former company had had a chance to repaint the butty in the fleet colours. The picture is taken at Marsworth top lock and the building in the background is a covered dry dock. The date is 30 April 1956.

191 During the latter part of the 1940s and early 1950s a few individuals started small carrying companies. Some used their war-time gratuities for the purchase of a few pairs of boats. All were convinced that there was still a good living to be made from canal carrying. One such was John Knill, later Sir John Knill. His pair of boats *Columba* and *Uranus* are seen in the top lock at Marsworth on the Grand Union Canal in November 1951. John Hemelryke poses for the photographer, Philip Weaver, also a crew member, while John Knill works the lock. Both boats were ex-Grand Union Canal Carrying Company fleet, bought from H. Dean of Manchester.

191

192 One of the greatest efforts to bring back narrowboat carrying in Britain was made by Leslie Morton when he formed the Willow Wren Canal Carrying Company. Leslie Morton had previously been manager of the Grand Union Canal Carrying Co's fleet, so he knew the business, and along with his financial backer, Captain Vivien Bulkeley-Johnson, they started carrying with a pair of boats in 1954. This photograph was taken at 6.30am in August 1954, and shows two ex-British Waterways boats which Willow Wren had purchased being taken from Bulls Bridge to Charity Dock at Bedworth for overhaul and re-fitting. The boats are the motorboats *Crane* and *Falcon* though only *Falcon* has power on. *Falcon* was shortly to be renamed *Sandpiper*. John Hemelryke and Philip Weaver were the crew. While Philip takes the photographs, John is at the bow and the motor boat is pushing open the top gate.

193 As Willow Wren expanded, so they required boatyard and docking facilities. They established the yard situated at the foot of the Braunston flight of locks, and here, in July 1959, there is much activity. *Teal, Crane* and *Sandpiper* are three of their five boats which appear in this photograph. Later they built a large shed alongside the

193

194

brick building seen here, complete with a sideways slip so they could pull boats up out of the water for repair under cover. The company was always in financial trouble, relying heavily on the generosity of Captain Vivien Bulkeley-Johnson. Later, a new company, Willow Wren Canal Transport Services Ltd, was formed in 1963, which leased boats from British Waterways and then hired them to the boatmen in return for a weekly rent, while the company contracted to try and find them cargoes. All failed in 1970, and the company stopped trading as a carrying firm.

194   In the north of England a new company, the Anderton Canal Carrying Company, sprang out of the remains of part of the Willow Wren Canal Transport Services Ltd fleet. This in turn had been part of a fleet formerly run by the north-western division of British Waterways. One of the first traffics obtained by the Anderton Canal Carrying Company in the summer of 1968 was that of moving silicaon carbide from Weston Point Docks to Norbury Junction for onward transmission by road to the Universal Grindingwheel Company of Stafford. While this cargo could be loaded cheaply overside in the docks, the unloading by mobile crane at Norbury, and subsequent road haulage to Stafford must have added considerably to the transport costs. The boatmen in this picture 'walking the plank' is 'Chocolate' Charlie Atkins, so named because for many years he carried chocolate crumb to Bournville on the Worcester and Birmingham Canal from Knighton on the Shropshire Union.

195   One of the most talked about carrying companies formed in recent year was the Birmingham and Midland Canal Carrying Co which came into being on the 8 March 1965. *The Times* reported on the 11 March '. . . for years Mr Waller and other inland waterway enthusiasts have been criticising British Waterways for pursuing a policy of allowing one of the world's best waterways systems to fall into ruin. Now they are backing their words with action, and such enterprise surely merits success.' While at first they were able to find sufficient trade to keep their fleets of boats operating, cargoes gradually diminished, and latterly the company has had to shift its emphasis on to the pleasure boat side of waterway business. Little is heard of the Birmingham and Midland Canal Carrying Co these days, except the occasional burst of acrimonious correspondence in the waterways press from a disgruntled shareholder. Here, one of their boats descends the locks at Stourport leading to the River Severn. This boat (with others) was making for Gloucester and then Sharpness, to load 75 tons of Polish timber for delivery to Warwick in May 1967. This was one of the traffics they tried to attract back to the canal system.

196   The steady decline in narrowboat trading came to an end in August 1970 when the celebrated coal run by the Blue Line Fleet from Atherstone to the Jam'ole at Southall stopped. For some time they had been the last regular long haul traffic, and then Kearley and Tongue closed the plant which was receiving the coal. Michael Streat who ran Blue Line Hire Cruisers from the ex-Samuel Barlow base at Braunston vowed he would keep some narrowboats trading even if they worked at a loss. When this traffic came to an end, he could find no more trade for his boats. Here a pair of Blue Line boats ascends the attractive flight of locks at Soulbury on the Grand Union Canal in February 1967.

197 In an effort to gain some publicity for the lack of maintenance on the canals due to their lack of finance, British Waterways embarked on a very controversial scheme to completely restore to perfect condition two miles of the Grand Union Canal around Tring. To this perfect piece of waterway they planned to bring sufficient VIPs to impress, in order that it might influence the future budget. The cost of this operation is reported to have been £200,000. As an added publicity stunt, two narrowboats from the Foxton Boat Company were used to bring 42 tons of stone from Peterborough to help with the work — some of it is seen being unloaded at the British Waterways depot at Bulbourne. The crew were Tony Clark and Bryan Allen, and the date is 15 October 1973. It seems ironic that British Waterways had to use two privately owned boats, as they had no suitable pairs of boats themselves. The Foxton Boat Company is one of a number of organisations who retain pairs of working boats in working trim. Most of the time they are lightly converted to carrying youth parties, and are known as camping boats. Motorboat *Baldock* and the butty *Virginis* are both ex-Grand Union Canal Carrying Co fleet. Behind the pair of boats are two interesting craft moored against the wharf. The smaller of the two is a weed cutter used to keep the growth of weeds in the canal down to a minimum. Behind is *Kingfisher* a former Grand Union Canal Company's inspection boat now used by British Waterways.

198 A new use for an old narrowboat. Besides being sold off to private traders, some were sold to the Thames Conservancy for a number of uses. Many people would think that this was a real come-down for a once proud and gaily painted trading boat, because, in this case, it has been converted for taking effluent from those Thameside

199

effluent disposal points which are not on a main sewerage system. This all-steel craft was one of the last built for trading on British Waterways and in fact is one of the ones fitted with the Harbormaster drive system. Here the boat is seen passing through a Thames lock.

199 In retirement, Rose Whitlock poses for the press photographer aboard the butty *Lucy* moored at Braunston. Rose, along with her husband Bill, was one of the crew of the famous Blue Line Fleet when they stopped trading in autumn 1970. Rose comes from a very old boating family. When this picture was taken on 17 April 1974 she and Bill lived aboard *Lucy* with Bill working at the nearby British Adhesives factory. Previously the butty *Lucy* was normally paired with the motorboat *Renfrew. Lucy* was originally built for John Knill and Son, and was launched at Barlow's Yard at Braunston early in 1952.

200 The stop lock at Autherly Junction outside Wolverhampton has a difference of only a few inches. For reasons best known to themselves, the fire brigade are pumping water from one level to another. The caption from the *Wolverhampton Express and Star* reads 'Even the canal gets traffic hold-ups . . . the Wolverhampton and District Fire Brigade are pumping water into the canal to raise the level and enable boats to proceed.' The date is 5 August 1953. Whatever the reason for this exercise, the point of including this picture is to show an almost empty stretch of water which nowdays is crammed with moored pleasure craft. There is now a boat-building yard and a hire boat base in the buildings on the left.

201 While the first hire boat business was set up on the Shropshire Union Canal by Mr G.F. Wain in 1935, the idea of letting out boats for holiday cruising on canals did not catch on in great numbers until the late 1950s. In the early years after World War II, it was difficult to find suitable hulls on which to build adequate cabin accommodation for cruising. One of the early firms in the business was the Canal Cruising Co of Stone, Staffordshire, under the leadership of R.H. Wyatt. Their first hire cruiser was the ex-fire float *Mancunian,* which they say was too high and apt to hit bridges. Here, in 1949, it passes two working boats, whose crew are obviously not used to seeing such odd craft. The hirers look apprehensive, even from astern, and just look at those clothes!

202 About this time people started selling ships lifeboats and ex-WD pontoons for conversion to private use. It was the well-known writer Tom Rolt who suggested to the Canal Cruising Company that as there was no shortage of old trading boats, it should be possible to cut these in half, adding a new bow to one half and a stern to the other.
The first butty, converted by S.E. Barlow's Yard at Tamworth, came out as the *James Brindley* and the *Angela* (named after Angela Rolt). In this photograph the original shape of the hull can be seen clearly. The boat on the wharf behind looks to have a most extraordinary superstructure.

203 Willow Wren Canal Transport Services Ltd ceased commercial carrying in 1970; though it had financial problems, the real reason was that it ran out of cargoes. Seeing the possibilities of hire boats as another form of income a number of working boat hulls were converted for cruising. The wooden butty *Kingfisher* formerly in the fleet of the earlier Willow Wren Carrying Company had lain idle in the reservoirs at Braunston for a long time. It was taken to Brownsover Wharf, Rugby, where, on 23 March 1968 workmen started to 'saw it in half'. From the way the boat is chocked it looks as if the two halves will fall on someone's toes.

204 British Waterways were not slow in starting up their own hire fleet and at first they too cut down old trading boats. For example, the working boat *Arabia* was cut down to 46ft in 1956 to become *Water Arabis* (to this day the Board's fleet are all named *Water* something). Most of these craft were converted to retain their tiller steering, but one or two were misguidedly given wheel steering from amidships. This is *Water Lilac* on the Lower Oxford Canal at Claydon in 1968. The coach windows of the earlier British Waterways conversions made it look very much like a bus! The spare battery on the stern deck was very necessary in the days before the alternator.

205 Some owners, of course, did not shorten the original 70ft hull but built a full length cabin on instead. Such boats could either form really luxurious accommodation for one family, or sleep up to ten or twelve in smaller cabins. This latter idea was the formula for the hotel boats. These boats usually worked as a pair, motor and butty, with accommodation for up to twelve people. One of the first firms in this business was Canal Voyagers of Preston Brook, and here their motorboat *Jupiter* and butty *Saturn* are passing a pleasure cruiser on the Macclesfield Canal in the late 1960s. The hotel boat is still very popular and caters for those people who want to see the countryside, but for one reason or another do not wish the responsibility of their own hire craft. *Saturn* is an ex-Shropshire Union Canal Carrying Company butty.

206 Already we have seen that working boats can be converted into camping boats quite easily, so that youth clubs and other organisations can have cheap holidays. Another version was the hostel boat. Here a horse-drawn, full-length working boat has been converted to give sparse cabin and living accommodation for young people. One of the fascinations of this boat *Pamela*, run by Hostel Craft, was the fact that it was kept as a horse-drawn boat and for many years it was pulled by a horse called Jim. Jim and *Pamela* are seen here on the Grand Union Canal late in the 1960s, just below Long Buckby bottom lock. It is interesting to note that over a period of six hours, the motor hire boat from which this picture was taken was only able to gain thirty minutes on the horse-drawn boat, and most of that was accounted for by Jim's lunch time! The reason for the rubbing stakes on the side of the bridge are clearly demonstrated in this picture.

207 Soon, firms were offering special steel hulls for pleasure boats built on old trading boat principles. Here the new meets up with the old, at Hawkesbury Junction, on the 18 April 1970. A brand new hire cruiser built by Harborough Marine of Market Harborough is on delivery to the British Waterways fleet at Nantwich in Cheshire. Moored up are three Birmingham and Midland Canal Carrying Co boats awaiting a cargo. By this time, however, their contracts for carrying coal were running out. The boats are moored close by the Greyhound — one of the best known of the canalside pubs. It is interesting to note that a working boat when fully loaded drew approximately four feet of water. Because of the lack of dredging and general maintenance these days, cruising boats are designed to draw less than two feet.

208 and **209** Back in 1961, British Transport Waterways were running down their own carrying fleet and as an organisation could not see what its future role would be. Trade was rapidly leaving the canals, and the real pleasure boating boom was ten years ahead. Old narrowboats were an embarrassment to the executive — they did not know what to do with them, except break them up. Selling to enthusiasts really was not worth the bother of the full tendering procedure, because prices were low. It was also fairly obvious that the executive did not really want boats on their waterways. Quite a number of narrowboats, mainly butties, were towed out to Harefield near Rickmansworth. Here a section of the bank was removed and the boats were floated into an adjacent gravel pit and scuttled. This act had not gone unnoticed, and letters were written to the press about this high level vandalism. British Transport Waterways denied the whole operation. Later, however, the water level in the gravel pits fell, leaving the boats exposed for all to see. It was at this time that these pictures were taken. The executive had to own up to its actions and later they made sure that the boats did not reappear, by covering them with spoil from the gravel pits. It must be clearly stated at this point that this sort of action would never have taken place if British Transport Waterways had the enthusiastic leadership which its successor, British Waterways Board, has at the time of writing. The motorboat seen on the right of Fig 209 is the ex-Fellows Morton & Clayton boat *Erica*.

210 For nostalgic and historic reasons, almost any 70ft ex-working boat is in demand these days. Often boats which had been given full length cabins are being bought and the cabins scrapped, leaving them with the original hull once again. Not so, as we have seen, in the late 1950s when you could hardly give them away. Many were scrapped or burned, or if there was a convenient resting place, they were sunk. Here, in a flash caused by brine pumping subsidence, near Northwich, dozens of boats were sunk, one on top of another according to eye witness reports. The hull in the foreground looks interesting, as it is not a traditional narrowboat in bow shape, and it has wheel steering at the stern. It is most probably an ex-Bridgewater Canal tug or one owned by a colliery company in the Manchester area. Wide boats capable of trading on the nearby River Weaver are also seen here, probably from the ICI fleet.

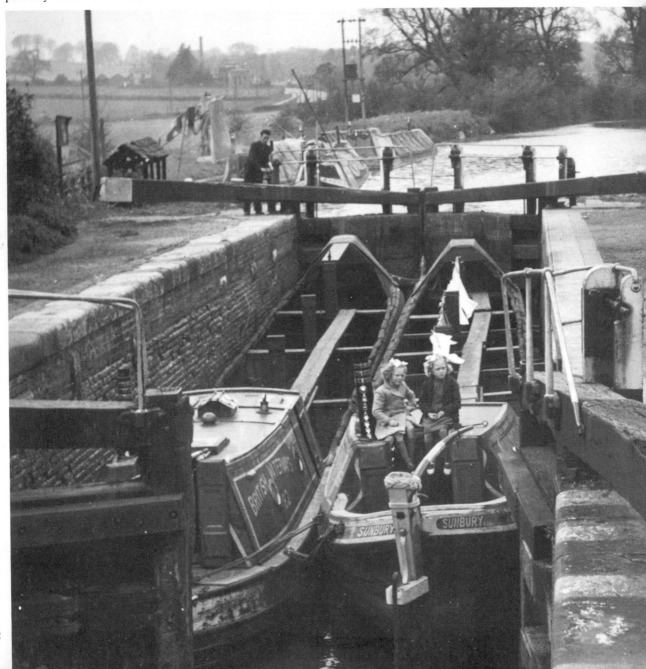

211 With the collapse of the Willow Wren Canal Transport Services Ltd in the late 1960s, British Waterways took back all the boats which they had leased to that company, and along with some of their own ex-trading fleet, moored them all in the reservoir (now a marina) at Braunston, to await further decision on their future. While it can be seen that no attempt was being made to protect them, it must be said that many of the boats were in a poor condition when taken back from Willow Wren. After lying here some time they were moved to Tringford on the Wendover branch of the Grand Union, and put up for sale. Practically all of them found buyers, and many have been restored back to full working order. This photograph was taken on 17 April 1970.

212 Motorboat *Tarporley* and butty *Sunbury* returning empty up country in Cow Roast Lock on the Grand Union Canal. Two loaded pairs are moored ahead of them. Will we ever see scenes like this again? No — original narrowboats are in very short supply, most of those which survive have been converted with full length cabins and fitted out for cruising. Those genuine working boats which are still in original trading condition are really only travelling museum pieces. Only a very few are still engaged in any form of trading — others cruise empty or with holds full of rowdy youth parties, when being used as camping boats. Most of the boats travelling on the canals over which narrowboats used to trade are now specifically built for leisure time cruising. While the narrowboat may have declined, the actual use of canals has increased greatly in recent years; in fact, some canals are busier now than in the hey-day of commercial trade.

INDEX